BRITISH BUSES
SINCE 1945

ALBERT SQ

40

VICTORIA PARK
BIRCH PARK
KINGSWAY

2150

CROSSLEY

JND 791

BRITISH BUSES SINCE 1945

John Creighton

BLANDFORD PRESS
Poole · Dorset

First published in the U.K.1983 by Blandford Press,
Link House, West Street, Poole, Dorset, BH15 1LL

Distributed in the United States by
Sterling Publishing Co., Inc.,
2 Park Avenue, New York, N.Y. 10016.

British Library Cataloguing in Publication Data

Creighton, John
  British buses since 1945.
  1. Buses—Great Britain—History
  I. Title
  629.2'2233'0941   TL232

ISBN 0 7137 1258 9

Set in 10/10½ point V.I.P. Plantin
by Polyglot Pte Ltd, Singapore.
Printed in Great Britain by Shenval Marketing Ltd.

Page 2
*Crossley H58R bodywork on a 1948 Manchester
Corporation Crossley DD42/8.*

Page 4/5
*Single deck Atkinson with Willowbrook coachwork
on the test track before delivery to North Western
Road Car Company.*

CONTENTS

*A Crosville (Wrexham) Bristol FS6G with Eastern
Coach Works body, built in 1965, pictured entering
Chester in 1981.*

INTRODUCTION

A number of changes in the multifarious aspects of the passenger vehicle scene, such as legislation, bus designs, fiscal situations, and mergers and closures of bus companies, have all contributed to making the post war years an interesting era. A salient feature of current times is the economic climate which has caused bus fares and the cost of new vehicles and fuel to spiral; together with a reduction in the 1982 transport supplement, this has forced many operators to review their services in an effort to win back passengers. The concern expressed by bus operators is typified by London Transport's statement in 1981 that a thirty year trend towards fewer passengers was worsening, while the National Bus Company in 1980 reported that passenger journeys were down one hundred and thirty million compared to the previous year.

The years since 1945 have seen legislation playing a prominent role in passenger vehicle development. In 1950 the maximum permitted length of single deckers was increased from 27 ft. 6 in. to 30 ft. while the length of double deckers was allowed to be 30 ft. in 1956 and 36 ft. in 1961. Such legislation naturally affected the design of chassis and bodywork of passenger vehicles. E.E.C. Regulation 1463/70 stated that recording equipment must be installed and used in passenger carrying vehicles in the U.K., and the cost to U.K. operators to equip their fleets with the tachograph was considerable. Moreover, the E.E.C. based system of vehicle certification which took effect in 1982 again affected costs and organisation, since, for instance, it necessitated a change in garage rota maintenance.

Developments in bus design since 1945 have encompassed a variety of trends and innovations, making the post war years a fascinating period for the bus enthusiast, operator, and manufacturer alike. Among the proliferation of designs one can pick out a few notable types which can be said to have made an impact on the bus scene, with underfloor engines creating an interest in the late 1940s, whilst rear engined buses aroused considerable interest in the 1950s. The inception of integral designs again encouraged new thinking, and the one man operated bus gradually caused the demise of crew operated vehicles; for instance, London Country's last crew operated service was converted to one man operation in 1981. In recent years concepts such as articulated buses (*e.g.* with British Airways) have created an interest and although London Transport has shelved plans for its own prototype, the XRM, it may be that the mid 1980s will see this vehicle in passenger work.

Mergers and closures of bus companies and of manufacturers are features of the post 1945 period, with Scammell Lorries, for example, being acquired by Leyland Motors in the mid 1950s, and the A.E.C. Group (comprising Park Royal vehicles, Maudslay Motor Company and Transport Equipment–Thornycroft) being integrated with Leyland in 1962. Changes in organisation structure have played a major part in altering the bus scene. The early 1970s heralded the start of the National Bus Company, necessitating a 'corporate livery' for its vehicles, which abolished the colour schemes previously used by companies such as Midland Red and East Yorkshire. Then, some time later, local fleet names appeared on buses in the form of titles, including Reddibus (1975) for Midland Red vehicles in the Redditch area, and today Hants and Dorset, for instance, display local names with captions such as South Hants and Antonbus, while local identities for Crosville include Mid-Cheshire, Bws Llyn and De Cambria. The changes in livery and designations have provided bus enthusiasts with a colourful background to the new trends in chassis and body design, with amalgamations involving some considerable repainting of buses, as instanced by the 1968 Transport Act establishing Passenger Transport Authorities such as Merseyside, Tyneside, West Midlands and SELNEC (South East Lancashire and North East Cheshire), the predecessor of Greater Manchester Passenger Transport Executive.

The contemporary bus scene is punctuated by the impact of foreign vehicles on U.K. roads together with British buses being sold abroad, the early 1980s, for example, witnessing Leyland selling Atlantean AN68 vehicles to Singapore, while MCW and Leyland Olympians are on the roads of Hong Kong. Some foreign companies are firmly ensconced on the U.K. bus market with Volvo and Scania, for instance, providing double deckers for a number of U.K. fleets, and the ascendancy of these and other European makes would suggest an increase in overseas chassis makes on U.K. roads in the 1980s.

A.E.C.

Many people associate A.E.C. (Associated Equipment Company) with passenger transport in London owing to the large number of A.E.C. buses in service with this area over the years, but A.E.C. was also the manufacturer of fire engines, dumpers, railcars and tractors. Early examples of A.E.C. buses could be observed in the first part of the 1900s when vehicles were passed to the London General Omnibus Company, including the X and K types, followed by the STL and A.E.C. 663T(1930), 664T and Regal 4. The 2RT was in evidence during 1938, when A.E.C. also offered the 661T, a trolleybus version of the Regent double decker.

A.E.C.'s history is punctuated by mergers and takeovers including the co-operation with Leyland in 1946 to form the trolleybus company of British United Traction Limited, whilst a couple of years later, A.E.C. acquired Crossley and Maudslay. Ironically, A.E.C.'s biggest rival, Leyland, made overtures to merge in the 1960s. The merger was completed in 1962, but with A.E.C. carrying on in much the same way as before for some time after; the Renown, introduced in 1962, still displayed the A.E.C. crest.

Double Deck Buses

REGENT II Following the Second World War, A.E.C. proceeded with their already successful range of buses, introducing the 16 ft. 3 in. wheelbase Regent II double decker powered by an A.E.C. 7.7 litre oil engine, bodywork provided by a variety of companies including Park Royal, Eastern Coach Works, Burlingham and Weymann. Examples of authorities with the Regent II were Reading, Lowestoft and Liverpool. Although normally built in standard form, Midland Red requested a hundred chassis which had front wings equipped with a radiator hidden behind a full width, non-standard bonnet. Production of Regent II chassis ceased in 1947 by which time about seven hundred were in use by fleets in the U.K.

REGENT III In 1946 A.E.C. publicised its Regent III chassis by running one from London to Glasgow and this doubtlessly paid off since examples of authorities with A.E.C. Regent III buses were found in many parts of the country, such

An A.E.C. Regent II with Weymann bodywork, in service with Liverpool Corporation, 1947.

A.E.C. Regent III/East Lancashire Coachbuilders, supplied new to Bamber Bridge Motor Services (B.B.M.S.) in 1955, and later sold to Edwards of Lydebrooke.

as St. Helens and Eastbourne with their East Lancashire built lowbridge vehicles, Dundee, Devon General, Ipswich, Oxford and Reading.

This 'Provincial' Regent III was unveiled in 7 ft. 6 in. or 8 ft. widths with a 16 ft. 4 in. wheelbase, in the first year or so having A.E.C. 9.6 litre oil engines and 7.7 litre engines as options, the latter coming with a four speed sliding mesh gearbox and vacuum servo brakes. Changes in technical specifications included longer bodywork in 1950 and an improved gearbox two years later, this last development bringing about a change in chassis reference, the 9613A becoming the 9613S while the 6812A became the 6812S. The 6812S was seen in places such as Liverpool and Oxford, while 9613S chassis, equipped with Weymann H56R bodies, could be observed with Devon General. East Lancashire Coach Builders also supplied coachwork for Regent IIIs and Bamber Bridge Motor Services

(B.B.M.S.) was an example of an operator with such bodywork on its vehicles.

Regent III buses were readily distinguishable by their radiators which were mounted lower than on earlier A.E.C. models, while the plain bonnet top and side gave it a distinctive appearance. In March 1947 the Regent III series 2 chassis came on the scene, numbered 0961, with a new look, now having the A.E.C. chromium plated radiator and a modified 9.6 litre engine with an oil bath air cleaner, and the dynamo positioned on the side of the engine. Liverpool Corporation owned Regent IIIs with Saunders–Roe anodised aluminium bodywork which was left unpainted.

A.E.C. Regent III/Saunders-Roe, 1954, in service with Liverpool Corporation, carrying specially treated anodised aluminium panels.

REGENT III RT The close relationship between London Transport and A.E.C. was underlined by the large number of Regent III RT double deck buses acquired by the city — almost four thousand seven hundred. An A.E.C. 9.6 litre six cylinder engine provided power for this vehicle. Launched in 1945, a variety of bodywork firms supplied components, including Park Royal, Roe, Weymann and Craven. The pre-war II RT exhibited a chassis quite different from that of the Standard Regent with a low profile radiator and bonnet, and, although the pre-war and post war models were outwardly similar, there were several alterations in design, including less timber, in the III RT.

Painted green or red, the RT buses of London had a width of 7 ft. 5½ in., height of 14 ft. 3½ in. and a 16 ft. 4 in. wheelbase, and the bodywork firms of Saunders-Roe, Park Royal and

A.E.C. Regent III RT, with London Transport, 1952.

Weymann constructed RT buses of similar appearance, whilst those with Craven bodies were equipped with an extra window on ~~the~~ *both* ~~lower~~ decks instead of using the four window design preferred by other firms.

REGENT IV During 1950 A.E.C. tested an underfloor engined double decker bus, the 27 ft. long Regent IV of semi-integral design, powered by a 9.6 litre horizontally mounted engine. Bodywork was supplied by Crossley and the back loader went for trials with a number of authorities but lack of interest on their part forced A.E.C. to abandon any production plans and so the Regent IV was never observed in service.

REGENT V October 1954 witnessed the inception of the Regent V, which was of similar design to earlier Regents with the vertical front engine and half width cab, but differed in the design around the radiator, although the former exposed radiator design was also in use until 1960. There was a choice of front or rear entrance, and short and long wheelbase, early buses having 16 ft. 4 in. wheelbase, while those after 1956 had 18 ft. 7 in. wheelbases. The exterior appearance of Regent V buses varied, some retaining old style front ends, such as those in Leeds, while Liverpool and Rochdale favoured the more enclosed look. East Kent Road Car Company had about one hundred and fifty Regent V buses, some of which were later changed to one man operated vehicles, while South Wales employed buses with Marshall and Willowbrook coachwork. Vehicles were still in use in the early 1980s. Roe bodywork could be seen on a variety of Regent V vehicles including those with York Pullman Bus Company.

During the mid 1960s A.E.C., changed their AV 590 and AV 690 engines for new versions and the 11.3-litre AV 691 was employed in 1966 for use in Regent V buses. About this time titles were 3D2RA for monocontrol Regent Vs and 3D3RA for synchromesh buses. It is interesting to note that London Transport never bought Regent V vehicles. About two thousand six hundred Regent Vs were built, this model being A.E.C.'s final double deck bus, with East Kent's A.E.C. Regents ceasing their everyday bus duties in July 1981.

ROUTEMASTER The Routemaster was of semi-integral design with mechanical units placed on detachable subframes supported by the bodywork. A prototype was exhibited at the 1954 Commercial Motor Show at Earls Court. Two years later the vehicle entered service. Named R2RH by A.E.C., it featured a 9.6 litre engine, Monocontrol transmission, power steering and hydraulic brakes. The next prototype was equipped with an A.E.C. AV 590 9.6 litre engine as standard together with complete automatic transmission. An interesting aspect to this was that the driver could choose to have fully automatic or semi-automatic transmission. With a 16 ft. 10 in. wheelbase capable of carrying a body 8 ft. wide and 27 ft. 6 in. long, the Routemaster soon

A York Pullman Bus Company vehicle, 1957, with A.E.C. Regent V chassis and Roe bodywork.

attracted attention from fleet operators including Northern General (1964) — the only group outside London with the vehicle, their models receiving power from Leyland engines. It is worth noting aspects of Northern General's policy with respect to Routemaster. In 1972 this operator attempted to alter one for one man operation, using an accident damaged vehicle for conversion, but did not try it throughout the fleet. Northern General's Routemasters were 30 ft. long and came with a front entrance with room for seventy-two passengers, and displayed sliding ventilators in place of quarter drop windows. Towards the end of the 1970s withdrawals of Northern General's

12

A.E.C. Routemaster, London Transport in 1965.

Routemaster began, some being sold to London
Transport, others to private concerns, and the last
trip made by one was in December 1980.

British European Airways acquired sixty-five
short wheelbase Routemasters for London Airport Services with front entrances and facilities
for towing a luggage trailer, but all except these
and Northern General's fifty long wheelbase vehicles were in service with London Transport.
London Transport purchased front entrance
standard length Routemasters, built for British
European Airways, and designated them
RMA, working from Romford North Street
Garage before being used as staff and training
vehicles.

London's Routemasters

The Standard Routemaster bus entered full scale
production in 1959 and over two thousand examples of the RM were owned by London Transport, equipped with an A.E.C. 9.6 litre or Leyland 9.8 litre engine and Park Royal bodywork,
accommodating sixty-four people sitting down. In
1965 the RML saw service with London Transport, again carrying Park Royal body but, being
longer than the RM, it was equipped with an
A.E.C. 11.3 litre engine. London had about five
hundred of these vehicles, each carrying seventy-
two seats. London introduced front entrance
Routemasters (FRM) in 1967 with rear mounted
A.E.C. 11.3 litre engines and Park Royal bodies

seating forty-one people in the upper deck and thirty-one on the lower deck, and having a laden weight of 13.55 tonnes.

London gave its own designations to the many types of Routemaster it possessed. RMC referred to the coach equipped with platform doors and fluorescent lighting, which entered service in 1962 as a double decker, and a number of the forty-seven RMC buses were used for Green Line Coaches. London gave the title RCL to longer Routemasters seating thirty-six on the top deck and twenty-nine on the lower. Entering service in 1965, this model, as usual, exhibited Park Royal bodywork together with platform doors, parcel racks and fluorescent lighting as on the RMC. It is interesting to note that in 1964–65 London Transport acquired nine front entrance longer version Routemasters built for Northern General Transport, (RMF) these vehicles possessing Leyland 9.8 litre engines and seating forty passengers on the top deck and thirty-two on the lower deck.

BRIDGEMASTER A chassisless integral double decker, with a low overall height of 13 ft. 5½ in. and a central gangway on lower and upper decks, the Bridgemaster, was revealed jointly by A.E.C. and Park Royal in September 1956. The Bristol Lodekka was already proving a success as a low height double decker with a central gangway upstairs, and A.E.C. were anxious to meet this competition with the Bridgemaster, giving much of the work to A.E.C.'s associates, Crossley Motors, who possessed their own body building division. The 1956 Commercial Motor Show saw the launch of a prototype, many people referring to the new product as the Crossley Bridgemaster since it carried Crossley insignia and could be viewed on the firm's stand at the exhibition, but just after production proper commenced the A.E.C. name was given in place of Crossley's.

The half cab layout had a similar frontal appearance to the A.E.C. Regent V and the new 9.6 litre AV 590 engine was vertically mounted at the front with the vehicle featuring vacuum type brakes and four speed synchromesh gearbox plus a double reduction type rear axle with offset drive allowing the main shaft to be at a lower level than the hubs, so permitting a low floor level. Coming in either 16 ft. 6 in. or 18 ft. 10 in. wheelbases carrying 27 ft. 8in. or 30 ft. long bodies, the

Bridgemaster later had air brakes and air rear suspension as standard, vehicles with these modifications being known as B3RAs, while earlier models were designated MB3RA. The third version of the Bridgemaster, called the 2B3RA, had the forward entrance introduced in 1960 and an 18 ft. 4 in. wheelbase with the same technical specifications as the B3RA model. Only one hundred and seventy-nine were constructed, production ending in 1963. About ten fleets purchased the Bridgemaster. Liverpool and Oxford acquired examples of the Park Royal Bridgemaster, while East Yorkshire had a unique design feature in their Bridgemaster in that the body was tapered above the waistline thus facilitating travel under Beverley Bar. Other instances of operators with this A.E.C. double decker were Cardiff, Premier Travel Cambridge, and South Wales.

RENOWN The early 1960s were important years for A.E.C., one of the salient matters being the acquisition of the group by Leyland in 1962. Another was the introduction of the two axle low floor double deck bus, the Renown, whose independent front suspension and air bellows rear suspension were similar to those of the Routemaster. Designed to take over from the not over successful Bridgemaster, A.E.C.'s Renown had a similar appearance to its predecessor apart from the space beneath the driver's windscreen, the Bridgemaster having a front overhang of the coachwork permitting the cab front corner to carry on in an unbroken line to the bottom edge of the panelling, but the protrusion of Renown front mud guards prevented this.

3B3RA versions came with four speed synchronished gearboxes, whereas the 3B2RA models carried four speed direct selection epicyclic gearboxes. With an 18 ft. 3½ in. wheelbase the vehicle had an overall length of 30 ft. and could take either forward or rear entrance bodies. Some two hundred and fifty Renowns were manufactured during the production period 1962–67, with South Wales purchasing nineteen in the year after the model was launched. As usual a variety of body firms provided coachwork with West Bridgeford UDC's Renowns displaying East Lancashire bodywork while Rotherham and Nottingham employed Roe and Weymann coachwork respectively.

Single Deck Buses

REGAL I Realising the potential offered by private coach operators, in 1946 A.E.C. launched the Regal I chassis with a 17 ft. 6 in. wheelbase accommodating a body 27 ft. 6 in. long and 7 ft. 6 in. wide, and equipped with an A.E.C. 7.7 litre oil engine and a four speed sliding mesh gearbox. Similar to the Regent II, the Regal I had the same bonnet, front wings, gearbox, radiator and engine and both chassis facilitated easy maintenance, thus making the Regal I and Regent II popular with fleet operators, such as Potteries MT, whose Regal I vehicles had Brush coachwork.

REGAL III During 1935 the Regal II appeared. It had the first A.E.C. radiator with a pressed, chrome plated shell, and was fitted with a 7.7 litre engine and crash gearbox. In 1947 the Regal III was presented to the public as a 17 ft. 6 in. wheelbase single decker with four speed crash gear box; in the following year a sliding mesh four speed gearbox and friction clutch were offered as options. When the legal lengths of passenger vehicles were increased in 1950, the Regal III wheelbase became 19 ft. 3 in. in order to carry a 30 ft. body. A cast aluminium radiator was introduced in place of the earlier chromium plated model.

Regal III buses with half cab bodywork sported a traditional A.E.C. radiator, but the radiator was hidden in the full fronted models. Bodywork was supplied by a large number of companies for the many Regal III's used by authorities such as Devon General, Midland General, the City of Oxford and foreign buyers, including Lisbon, Portugal, and Uruguay.

REGAL IV The Regal IV — announced in 1949 and not to be confused with the pre-war Regal 4 — was the first production underfloor engine P.S.V. chassis in the U.K. With a 15 ft. 8 in. wheelbase for domestic markets and 17 ft. 6 in. for overseas buyers, the Regal IV U.K. model was referred to as the 9821E. London Transport was the only authority to acquire the 15 ft. 8 in. length, employing two dozen or so for private hire purposes, other groups favouring the 16 ft. 4 in. wheelbase introduced when the permissible overall length of single deckers was increased to 30 ft.

Utilising the 9.6 litre six cylinder engine in a horizontal position, the Regal IV was equipped with air brakes and a four speed pre-selective gearbox, a four speed synchromesh gearbox with friction clutch being offered as an option in 1951. The 9821E chassis featured a fluid flywheel and epicyclic gearbox, while a friction clutch and four speed synchromesh gearbox came on the scene during 1952, referred to as 9821S and 9822S.

In spite of a somewhat heavy chassis compared to those used by competitors, the Regal IV was popular in several areas, including Thomas Tilling's coaches (with Eastern Coach Works bodies for their 9821E models) operating in and around London, while Douglas Corporation favoured Willowbrook 9822E versions, and 9822E Regal IV/Park Royal vehicles were in service with London Transport, Oxford and Ipswich Corporations.

RELIANCE The very successful Reliance underfloor engined single deck chassis was really the result of tests by A.E.C. to find a lighter chassis than the one employed for the Regal IV, and 1953 witnessed the company's introduction of a popular chassis receiving power from either A.E.C.'s 6.75 litre or 7.7 litre oil engines, clutched to a five speed synchromesh gearbox. From 1961 onwards a larger AH 590 engine was used and towards the end of the 1960s six speed synchromesh and six speed direct air operated epicyclic gearboxes were made available.

There were several designations for chassis types: the MU2RA had epicyclic transmission; MU3RA featured vacuum brakes and synchromesh; MU3RV referred to Reliances with air brakes and synchromesh gearboxes, while the MU3RAE was an export model. During 1961 the 18 ft. 7 in. wheelbase and 36 ft. long bodywork appeared together with a new engine in the form of the AH 590 model and this chassis type was referred to as 2U3RA; the 18 ft. 7 in. chassis with the AH 691 11.3 litre engine was known as the

A.E.C. Regal IV/Willowbrook, the first underfloor engined bus in the City of Oxford, 1952 (top right).

Alexander bodywork on an A.E.C. Reliance (1961) owned by Scottish Omnibuses (bottom right).

6U3R2, and those equipped with four speed direct air operated transmission were designated 6U24. When the Southall factory finally closed in 1978 the Reliance ceased to be produced and about that time the title 'Leyland Reliance' replaced the A.E.C. insignia on vehicles.

During 1960 London Transport acquired three vehicles with A.E.C. 2MU2RA chassis and these Reliances were fitted with Willowbrook coachwork having separate entrance and exit for use as one man operated buses in rural areas, but these single deckers were not popular with drivers and they were later sold to Chesterfield Corporation. London also tried out fourteen A.E.C. Reliances for use on Green Line routes, based at Dunton Green and Windsor, features including panoramic windows and head rests, seating for forty-nine

A.E.C. Reliance/Plaxton new to Burnetts of Mintlaw, later passing to Alexander Northern, and withdrawn in 1980.

and an overall length of 36 ft., power coming from an A.E.C. AH 691 six cylinder oil engine with coachwork by Willowbrook.

Many Reliances saw service in coach operation, such as Alexander bodied vehicles with Scottish Omnibuses, while others were employed by transport authorities such as Devon General whose models were unusual in that they had offside doors to the driver's cab, while examples of MU2RA vehicles with Weymann bodies were seen in Hull Corporation Transport Department. MU3RVs were used by East Kent and Maidstone

A.E.C. Reliance/Marshall B45F body, built in 1969, seen in the last few months of Reliance operation with Alder Valley.

and District, and Grimsby Corporation; South Wales (Willowbrook B53 F models); Rochdale, whose forty-two seat dual door models carried East Lancashire bodywork; MacBraynes, with Duple coachwork; Neath and Cardiff Luxury Coaches, with Plaxton bodywork; Alder Valley, where some Reliances had Marshall coachwork. There are still some examples of Reliances in use although many are now being removed from fleets — in 1981–82 East Kent withdrew several Reliance vehicles as did Reading (numbers 251–4) and South Wales (Plaxton DP51F models.)

MONOCOACH During 1953 A.E.C. manufactured a new range of medium weight vehicles including the Mercury truck, the Reliance bus/coach chassis and the Monocoach — an underfloor engined integrally constructed single deck bus chassis, with many components identical to those used in the Reliance. Built in conjunction with Park Royal, the Monocoach had a 16 ft. 4 in. wheelbase and an AH 410 6.8 underfloor mounted engine, being designated MC2RA with air brakes and Monocontrol transmission, while vehicles with vacuum brakes were known as MC3RV, and MC3RA referred to chassis supplied with synchromesh gearboxes.

The Monocoach was an attempt by A.E.C. to construct a light single deck bus, but in fact it was only slightly lighter than the Reliance and just three hundred and fifty-nine were manufactured, some seeing service with Northern General whose twenty-four Monocoaches had Park Royal bodies, while other instances of this integrally constructed bus could be found with Sheffield and Scottish Omnibuses authorities.

SWIFT AND MERLIN The 1961 legislation allowing the use of 36 ft. long buses encouraged several new models such as Bedford's VAL and Bristol's RE chassis. A.E.C. demonstrated the Swift single decker at the 1964 Commercial Motor Show, displaying a rear horizontal engine on a low frame or high frame chassis, intended for urban work and coach work respectively, the latter having underfloor space in place of the usual rear luggage boot. Buyers could choose either 16 ft. 6 in. or 18 ft. 6 in. wheelbase versions for 33 ft.

or 36 ft. long bodies while a choice of engines was presented between the A.E.C. AH 505 or AH 691 11.3 model, and further options included a four or five speed gearbox. The popularity of Swifts was reflected in the number of operators using the bus, such as Nottingham and Blackpool whose fleet included forty-seven seat Marshalls-bodied types, while East Lancashire supplied coachwork for Swifts in service with Southampton and Ipswich Corporation Transport. Transfers and withdrawals have taken place between authorities; during the early 1970s West Midlands PTE sold

A.E.C. Swift carrying Willowbrook forty-eight seat bodywork which came into service with South Wales in September 1969 and was transferred to London Country Bus in May 1971.

Swifts with Strachan bodies to Northampton, and in the early 1980s Grampian withdrew Alexander-bodied Swifts from their fleet.

As usual London Transport were loyal to A.E.C. and in 1970 purchased forty-four SM single deck Swift one man operated buses with room for forty-six seated passengers, a single front entrance/exit, Marshalls' body and rear mounted A.E.C. AH 508 8.2 litre engine. London's SMS buses, introduced in 1980, were Swift one man operated vehicles with front entrance and centre exit, provision for thirty-three people sitting down and thirty-four standing. About two hundred of these buses were on London's roads in the early 1970s.

Constant mesh and semi-automatic gearboxes were introduced with the larger 11.3 litre AH 691 engine and London Transport gave the name of Merlin to these vehicles, equipping them with low driving positions which were later raised following complaints from drivers. Referring to Merlins as MBAs, London Transport had sixty-nine on the road and these multi-standing buses

A.E.C. Swift/Northern Counties, Nottingham City Transport, 1970.

accommodated twenty-eight seated and forty-eight standing passengers on the Red Arrow service. The bodywork, with separate entrances and exits, came from Metropolitan–Cammell–Weymann. In 1966 London put into service six A.E.C. Merlins with Strachan bodies on routes such as the Victoria to Marble Arch run, and their popularity was reflected in the purchasing of a further nine with Strachan bodies, painted green and featuring separate entry and exit points.

SABRE The 1968 Sabre single deck chassis had a 20 ft. wheelbase and an overall length of 38 ft. 2 in. and was equipped with an 800 series V8 13.1 litre engine. It had many features of the Swift in its design. In spite of coil spring suspension and hydraulic dampers on both axles the Sabre, or VP2L, was not a success and less than ten were manufactured.

A.E.C. Swift 3MP2R/Marshall, built in 1975 for Blackpool Corporation (right).

A.E.C. Merlin/Metropolitan–Cammell–Weymann (M.C.W.) seen on the Red Arrow Service, London Transport, 1970 (below).

ALBION

Pre 1945 Albion buses included the PB24, PH24, and the PM28 which came on the scene in 1926 as a forward control chassis with an Albion four cylinder petrol engine. The PW65 of 1931 was a forward control single deck chassis, also powered by an Albion engine, while the 1931 Valiant PV70 could seat thirty-two passengers. Some Albion models from before 1945 continued in production after the war, with the CX9 (1937), CX13 and CX19 being examples. About four hundred CX19 Venturers were made between 1938 and 1949, driven by an Albion 8.4 litre six cylinder unit, and later a 9.08 litre model. The CX13 Valkyrie chassis originally came on the bus scene in 1937, manufacture ceasing in 1940, but starting again in 1946. It was a forward control chassis with standard transmission, a four speed constant mesh gearbox and vacuum servo assisted brakes. South Yorkshire had examples, while those in service with Glasgow differed slightly from the original model and were known as CX25s.

Six months after the 1950 Motor Show at Earls Court it was announced that Leyland Motors and Albion Motors had amalgamated, Albion being one of Scotland's last remaining motor manufacturers.

VENTURER CX37 The CX37 double decker chassis, introduced in 1947, had a wheelbase of just over 16 ft. and an overall length of 26 ft. It was seen on Glasgow streets with Croft H56R bodywork, while Western had vehicles with Alexander bodywork. In 1947 a six cylinder 120 bhp version of the smaller 105 bhp oil engine was announced and this was put into the Venturer double decker with a four speed constant mesh gearbox.

VENTURER CX39N In 1947, realising the potential of the single decker market, Albion decided to bring out the CX39N, a single deck chassis with forward control and a 17 ft. 6 in. wheelbase. Independent operators together with municipal authorities expressed an interest in this vehicle. Economic of Whitburn had examples with Associated Coachbuilders chassis type C33F, while Duple bodywork was seen upon a coach owned by Hutchinson of Overtown. The CX39N was powered by the Albion EN 243B six cylinder

9.9 litre engine. Although a popular chassis type, production ended after three years in 1950.

VICTOR The most popular Albion passenger vehicle was the Victor. The pre-war version possessed a dropped chassis frame featuring raised wheel-arches, but post-war versions had straight chassis frame. The FT 39N came on the transport scene in 1947 with a 15 ft. 11½ in. wheelbase and Albion oil engine whilst the FT 3AB was powered by the Albion six cylinder 4.3 litre petrol model. The FT 39 and FT 3AB differed from pre-war models in that the radiator was more angular, carrying the Albion's rising sun symbol. Albion's FT 21N model was launched in 1949 as a forward control chassis whose wheelbase measured 11 ft. 9 in., but it was not very successful and remained in production for only one year.

During 1951 a modified FT 39 was introduced in the form of the FT 39AN which had a 16 ft. wheelbase and a slightly longer rear overhang with facilities for a dropped rear frame extension, while three years later the FT 39AL, with the longer 16 ft. 11½ in. wheelbase, appeared. The introduction of bigger 5.5 litre oil engines caused the designation to be altered to FT 39 KAN and FT 39 KAL in 1956, and three years later witnessed the end of FT 39 types.

1959 saw two new chassis replace the FT 39 series, though still retaining the name Victor. Full sized vehicles accommodating up to thirty-seven and forty-one passengers, they were known as VT 15 AN and VT 15 AL, but when provided with a Leyland 0.370 six cylinder oil engine they were named VT 17 BN and VT 17 BL.

Albion Victors could be found in service in places such as Guernsey where Watson's Greys owned an FT 39 AN, the fleet of this operator having only seven buses including five Albion Victors and an Albion Nimbus, while MacBraynes had some pre-war PHC49 Victors with Park Royal bodywork, first licensed in 1933, and later sold to Brown Brothers of Glasgow.

VIKING In 1948 Albion's Viking chassis was offered to bus operators in the form of a single deck unit with a 9.9 litre 120 bhp engine providing power. Albion's biggest single decker and a popular export vehicle, the Viking came in a variety of forms. The CX 41 LW had a 20 ft. 6 in.

Albion CX19/Eastern Coach Works, with Red and White Motor Service (top left).

Albion CX37S/Alexander, a fifty-three seater built in 1949 and owned by Western S.M.T. Company Ltd (below left).

Albion Victor FT39N/Alexander, built in 1950 with seating for thirty-two (above).

wheelbase while the CX 41 NW had an 18 ft. 3 in. wheelbase, catering for overall bus lengths of 33 ft. and 30 ft. respectively; the HD 61LW, whose width was 8 ft., had a 21 ft. wheelbase and 37 ft. overall length. Such lengths were mainly for overseas use. Domestic fleets had examples of the HD 61N chassis, which appeared in 1950, with a 19 ft. wheelbase, overall length of 30 ft. and width of 7 ft. 6 in. The HD 61 NW chassis was the same as the former except that it measured 8 ft. in width.

Manufacturer of the Viking Series ended in 1951 by which time several fleets, particularly in Scotland, had examples. The early 1980s saw some withdrawn from service, such as an Albion VK 43L Viking with Alexander C40F bodywork, which had been in service with Alexander (Midland).

OTHER ALBION SINGLE DECKERS The KP7 1 NW came on the market in 1952 as a single deck chassis with 16 ft. 4 in. wheelbase and horizontally placed engine of the Albion eight cylinder 9.7 litre variety. Three years later the company introduced the Nimbus MR9N single deck underfloor engine chassis, powered by an Albion four cylinder 3.83 litre engine. Albion's prototype underfloor engined chassis of 1955 had the conventional radiator in view but when the production model of this Aberdonian (MR 11L) came on the market two years later the radiator was positioned in a manner similar to that of the Nimbus, tilted at about 47 degrees. Aberdonian single deckers had 16 ft. 4 in. wheelbases, a Leyland 5.8 litre oil engine, a five speed constant mesh gearbox, and vacuum hydraulic brakes.

Guernsey was among the areas operating the Albion Nimbus NSSN, which made its début in

1958 as a replacement for the Nimbus MR9, having a larger 4.1 litre engine. Two years later the NS3AN appeared, equipped with a five speed constant mesh gearbox and displaying a dropped extension behind the rear springs as an option.

LOWLANDER The Lowlander was a low height double deck design capable of taking bodies with up to seventy-four seats. An overall height of 13 ft. 6 in. was possible because of the cranked frame layout. A Leyland 140 bhp diesel engine was standard, while choices were offered between synchromesh or semi-automatic gearboxes, and leaf spring or air rear suspension. The range of Lowlanders included the LR1, LR2 and the LR5 and LR7; the last two came on the market in 1962, and had an overall height of only 13 ft. 3⅞ in. After four years of making this bus, Albion ceased manufacture of the Lowlander in 1965. Southend Corporation and Fife are two instances of companies running the Lowlander.

A 1962 Albion Lowlander/Alexander with Fife Ltd.

An A.E.C. Reliance 2U3RA/Plaxton
'Highwayman' of 1963, now privately owned, but
formerly with L.U.T. (1963–74) (above).

A.E.C. Reliance formerly with Premier Travel,
Cambridge, (below left); 1963 Albion Lowlander
LR1 of Alexander (Northern) (below); both are
Alexander-bodied.

A Bedford YRQ carrying 49 seat Willowbrook 'service' body. Now privately owned, it was originally with W. Alexanders & Sons (Midland).

This Bedford YMT/Alexander spent many years with Lothian Region Transport before being sold to a Cheshire coach firm.

Bedford VAM, with a 193 in. wheelbase for forty-one/forty-five seater applications.

Bedford VAS (164 in. wheelbase) featuring Duple bodywork with 214 cu. in. petrol or 300 cu. in. diesel engines available (above).

A Bedford CF minibus on a CF van chassis (below).

A line up of Bristol RE coaches with Plaxton coachwork powered by Gardner 150 and Leyland 680 engines (above).

Eastern Coach Works seventy-four seater of 1978, in service with Crosville (below).

Bristol L6B/Beadle C32R built in 1949 for Wiltshire and Dorset.

Built in 1967 for Hants and Dorset, this Bristol FLF6L/Eastern Coach Works vehicle is powered by a Leyland 0.600 engine and is currently owned by a school in Stockport (above).

A B.U.T. 961 IT/Weymann H56R built in 1951 seen here with Bradford City Transport (below).

Metropolitan-Cammell-Weymann bodywork is carried on this 1967 Daimler Fleetline CRG6LX with Greater Manchester P.T.E. livery.

Two Daimler CVG6 double deckers, built in 1958, both carrying Metropolitan–Cammell H33/27R bodywork and seen here on the road in West Midlands P.T.E. livery and former Coventry colours.

A Daimler COG5/Willowbrook coach (GNU 750) built in 1939 and seen with Blue Bus Company, and a Daimler CVD6/Duple (1950).

Daimler Fleetline CRG6LXB with Roe bodywork, built in 1976 for the private operator, Mayne (above).

Two Ford R1114 coaches with Plaxton Supreme bodywork (below).

ATKINSON

ALPHA PM Passenger chassis formed quite a small part of Atkinson's vehicle production, buses not making an appearance until 1950 when the Alpha PM arrived. A single decker with underfloor Gardner engine, examples were owned by Sunderland Corporation, North Western Road Car Company and a number of private operators. The PM 746H featured a 16 ft. 6 in. wheelbase and the 6HLW engine while the PM 745H chassis (1952) carried the 5HLW unit.

ALPHA PL The early 1950s saw Atkinson's PL 74 range on the market, accommodating a 30 ft. body and offering a choice of Gardner

A 1953 Atkinson Alpha in service with Lancashire United, carrying Northern Counties coachwork.

4HLW, 5HLW or 6HLW engines, SHMD (a north western bus group) being an example of a company employing this light underfloor engine single decker.

PD 746 It is interesting to note that only two chassis for the PD 746 double decker were constructed, both powered by the Gardner 6LW oil engine. SHMD was the bus company operating the PD 746. The *Commercial Motor* of August 1954 refers to the 'unusual gearbox mounting arrangement in new chassis' of the PD 746: the gearbox had a three point mounting and, instead of the David Brown 557 unit attached straight on to the clutch housing, a flat full width bracket was bolted to the face of the box, supporting Metacone units carried by a tubular cross-member placed ahead of the box.

AUSTIN

Before 1945 Austin made quite a few ventures into the passenger vehicle sector, the K2 and K4 chassis of 1939, for example, being forerunners of models in the late 1940s.

CXB In March 1947 the Austin CXB normal control model chassis came on the market. With a 15 ft. wheelbase and an overall length of 25 ft., it was powered by a $3\frac{1}{2}$ litre Austin six cylinder petrol engine. It served with companies such as Beestons of Hadleigh, and Pollard in Cornwall. In 1948 two developments occurred in the CXB production, a forward control version was introduced to the public, referred to as the 'coach' chassis, and a 4 litre six cylinder Austin engine was offered to customers. A number of bodywork builders showed interest in the CXB, and popular CXB/body combinations included vehicles with Plaxton, Mulliner and Mann Egerton coachwork allowing up to thirty passengers to be seated.

CXD A further chassis of 1948, the CXD possessed a 15 ft. wheelbase and either a Perkins or Austin 4 litre six cylinder engine. Some CXD coaches had Metalcraft and Kenex bodywork.

The 'K' Series

K8 While operators were purchasing the CXB, Austin pressed on with further developments including the K8 forward control chassis, which came on the market as a passenger or commercial model powered by the company's 2.2 four cylinder engine.

K2SL During 1948 the Austin K2SL made its début. A commercial vehicle chassis adapted for passenger vehicle use by a number of firms, it had an Austin 4 litre six cylinder petrol engine and four speed gearbox, the K2SL's wheelbase measuring 11 ft. 2 in., but it was only manufactured for just over one year.

K4SL Once again this chassis was also employed in goods vehicles but some coachbuilders, including Whitson, utilised the K4SL for passenger vehicles in 1948, the chassis remaining in production for two years. During 1952 the Austin and Morris groups merged and they stopped producing passenger chassis for domestic operators.

BEADLE

Dartford, Kent was the home of Beadle Coach-builders who made a small number of prototype single deckers in 1946 from light alloy materials, consequently reducing the weight of the finished product and so improving fuel consumption. Using parts from different companies, Beadle buses were on the roads with various components from Leyland Cub, Titan and Tiger models together with Commer engines, and during the early 1950s Beadle made buses with A.E.C. Regent parts. Some examples of operators with Beadle buses included Southdown, East Yorkshire and East Kent, who acquired about thirty of the thirty-nine seat vehicles.

BEDFORD

During 1931 Bedford unveiled their first bus and coach chassis and by the end of the year the company was responsible for over half of the fourteen to twenty seater coach market in Britain, preparing the way for a distinguished time in bus and coach production. Pre 1945 passenger vehicles included WHB and WLB chassis models in the 1930s, the 1935 WTB chassis for twenty-six seat coach/bus bodies, and the famous Bedford OB single deck bus chassis which was introduced in 1939 and stayed in production until the early 1950s by which time some twelve thousand seven hundred had been constructed. 1942–45 was the manufacturing period for the Bedford OWB whose features were governed by war austerity, resulting in a bus with wooden slatted seats. The war years also witnessed the OLAZ(1939–53), a modified version of the OL goods chassis. Lesser known Bedford passenger vehicles, such as the J2 — based on a truck chassis — and the M type chassis, could be observed with some domestic operators and also in foreign markets.

SB At the Commercial Motor Show in 1950 Bedford announced the new range of S goods vehicles incorporating the SB passenger chassis whose features included a 206 in. wheelbase — the longest Bedford chassis at the time — and a new Bedford petrol engine. (Bedford tend to give their vehicle dimensions in inches.) Early SB bodies were thirty-three seat models and of the first body makers to show an interest, Duple was in the forefront, in 1953 announcing a new style of Vega body for the vertical engined Bedford SB, without the bulbous front of early Vega vehicles. Operators were attracted to the Bedford SB/Duple Vega with its thirty-three/thirty-eight seats, curved front corner glasses and improved side mouldings. Soon the Vega Coach and Bedford/Duple Mark VI bus were common sights on U.K. and foreign roads. The SB chassis was in service with New Zealand and Portuguese

Bedford OB with Duple bodywork, built in 1948.

companies. Perspex panels in the roof dome could be observed in Duple vehicles popular with U.K. firms such as Fountain Coaches.

It could be argued that the Commer Avenger was a rival to the SB chassis during the early 1950s and Bedford introduced a variety of modifications to enhance the SB's place on the market; at first powered by a Bedford 4.93 six cylinder petrol engine the model was re-fitted with a Perkins 5.6 litre oil engine in 1953 and later a Bedford six cylinder 4.93 oil engine, a Leyland 0.350 5.8 litre six cylinder oil unit and, in 1961, the Bedford six cylinder 5.4 litre oil engine.

During the years of production, 1950–73, almost thirty thousand SB versions of Bedford chassis were constructed with a number of body types including Plaxton who introduced a thirty-three seater in 1951, Thurgood whose model accommodated thirty-five or thirty-seven people, and Burlingham. Later models were designated by numbers, such as SB5 which replaced the SB1 in 1961, and the SB13 which had hydraulic air brakes while five speed synchromesh gearboxes became available for SB coaches in 1963.

Bedford SB/Duple Vega, twenty-eight seater (1952) with East Kent.

OLAZ The SB was undoubtedly popular but some operators asked for a smaller coach/bus chassis, and to accommodate this demand Bedford introduced the OLAZ in the early 1950s, a modified version of the OL goods chassis. Powered by a six cylinder petrol engine the OLAZ had a 157 in. wheelbase. It was immediately popular with coach operators, including McBrayne whose fleet included OLAZ coaches with Duple B20F bodies. Duple also employed an interesting Sportsman coach whose body had plywood side panels on an exposed timber framework and an OB Vista bonnet.

VAS In 1950 Bedford inaugurated the 300 cu. in. engine whose popularity was reflected in its being used in a new chassis which appeared in August 1961, the VAS, also powered by the Bedford 214 cu. in. petrol unit. The larger SB chassis was an outstanding success but some fleet owners wel-

Bedford VAS/Duple Vista 25 with National Cash Register, 1970.

comed the smaller VAS chassis, used in twenty-nine/thirty seat vehicles, and foreign operators, such as in Cyprus, found the new chassis ideal for their purposes. On the domestic front, VAS coaches were seen with East Midland whose Vista 28 bodied vehicles proved an ideal smaller bus, and SELNEC had a couple of Vista bodied VAS buses, while the famous Duple Dominant coachwork was suitable not only for larger chassis but also for VAS chassis. Duple Vista 25 coachwork could also be observed with VAS coaches owned by National Cash Register.

Specifications for the VAS included a 164 in. wheelbase and 16 in. wheels pioneered by Bedford allowing for low floor height and consequently improving access to vehicles for passengers. The VAS was equipped with a transmission handbrake and superior braking system in line with those on TK trucks, further promoting Bedford in the passenger vehicle market.

C TYPE The arrival of another small coach to meet demands of certain operators took place in the 1950s with Bedford offering a twenty-nine seat luxury coach based on the C type truck chassis, a four ton forward control model. With the name 'New Vista', this bus was available in 8 ft. or 7 ft. 6 in. wide versions. The Duple twenty-nine seat coach was, in fact, a smaller version of the Vega but did not have a wrap round rear window and had a heart shaped grill. About this time the success of Bedford was underlined by the one millionth Bedford built in 1958. About three hundred and sixty thousand had been exported. 1958 was also the year a service bus body was constructed for the Bedford C 5Z1 chassis, a shorter thirty seat model of the Duple (Midland) bus body whose high window line came down at the front, joining with the bottom of the windscreens.

The Bedford CA Series remained in production from 1952 to 1969. It was replaced by the CF, a range which included a model with Plaxton seventeen seat bodywork, and the twelve seat Utilabus — a converted CF van, used, for instance, by W. Sutherland in the Isle of Skye

during the 1960s—while Reeve Burgess bodied seventeen seaters proved popular with many operators.

VAL The transport market was attracted to the VAL chassis, introduced in 1962 as a three axle single deck vehicle with four wheel steering and a 17 ft. 8 in. wheelbase and overall length of 36 ft. As though to remind the public that Bedford catered for larger seating capacities in addition to the smaller models such as the VAS, the company aimed its VAL chassis at fifty-five seat body coaches, and the good turning circle plus powered steering made it popular with coach drivers.

The 16 in. diameter wheels permitted a low body line so aiding boarding and alighting. The original engine was the Leyland 0.400 diesel conventionally situated at the front, with a five speed synchromesh overdrive gearbox and hypoid rear axle. Perhaps the high acclaim for this marque could in some way be attributed to the fact that Bedford designed the VAL chassis specifically for use as a passenger carrying vehicle, rather than adapting existing lorry chassis such as the OB and SB models based on the O type truck and S type truck designs.

Operators were impressed by the economic price of VAL chassis (in 1962, only £1,775) and the door forward of the front axle — although the SB chassis had been adapted by a Loughborough firm, the VAL was in fact the first Bedford bus/coach chassis with this forward positioned door. A number of body firms used the VAL chassis, including Plaxton, whose Embassy II had fifty-two seats, Metropolitan–Cammell–Weymann with the Topaz, and Duple, whose Vega Major featured panoramic windows in a fifty-two seater model. Examples of companies employing VAL chassis in their buses included Kenzies of Cambridgeshire, Trans World Airways at airports, Barton, and the North Western Road Car Company. It is interesting to note that in 1965 the fifty thousandth Bedford passenger chassis was a VAL which was sent to Australia. In 1967

Bedford YNT with Dominant III coachwork, used for express work (top left).

Bedford VAL, built in 1962 with a 231 in. wheelbase (bottom left).

the VAL chassis was provided with the Bedford 466 cu. in. diesel engine. Among the last Bedford VAL's to be constructed, were models with Duple Viceroy thirty-six seat coachwork (fifty-three passengers) delivered to Webbs of Armscote in the early 1970s, when production of VAL chassis ceased.

VAM The mid 1960s saw Bedford bring the VAM chassis to the coach and bus scene, a medium wheelbase passenger unit capable of taking front entrance bodies, having a 193 in. wheelbase and forty-one/forty-five seats. Examples of firms utilising coaches on VAM chassis included Stardust coaches, one man operated vehicles with Hants and Dorset (Strachan body), Highland Omnibus (Alexander body), Irvins of Law, Lloyds of Begilt, and Grayline. Bedford provided three engines for the VAL chassis — the company's own 300 cu. in. and 330 cu. in. diesel models and the Leyland 0.400 diesel engines. Several body manufacturers adopted the VAL chassis for their requirements — Strachans, for instance, produced the Pacesaver 11, while Duple designed the Viscount specifically for VAM chassis, similar to the Commander, available with both sliding and fixed windows and accommodation for forty-five passengers, and the Portuguese company of Salvador Caetano supplied the Cascais on the VAM chassis with distinctive styling.

YRQ At the onset of the 1970s the VAL twin steer chassis was discontinued and Bedford presented its first underfloor engined coach/bus chassis, the YRQ, a 16 ft. wheelbase, forty-five seater vehicle with several features from the VAM series. Powered by a Bedford 466 cu. in. diesel engine the chassis was equipped with a five speed overdrive gearbox and offered some considerable passenger comfort since the mid ships, underfloor engine position reduced noise level, while the ease of entry and exit encouraged operators to use the YRQ chassis for one man operated services. Examples of YRQ vehicles could be seen with Isle of Man National Transport (Willowbrook bodies), Edinburgh City Transport with a forty-four seater Duple Viceroy body and Wright coaches who also favoured Plaxton bodywork.

YRT An 18 ft. 5 in. wheelbase chassis, the YRT,

Bedford YRQ with Plaxton bodywork, owned by Wright Brothers 1980.

was exhibited by Bedford in 1972 to cater for larger coaches in demand by coach and bus operators. The YRT was capable of carrying fifty-three seat bodies with power coming from a 466 cu. in. engine, positioned mid ships. As usual, coachwork was provided by a number of companies, including Plaxton and Willowbrook, whose 002 'Express Bus' body had a sleek appearance. Duple's name for bodywork on the YRT fifty-three seat chassis was 'Dominant' — a salient part of Duple's history because this was the first time an all steel structure was available for use on light and heavyweight chassis — which featured closer pitched body pillars, curved glass windows, and a double curvature two piece windscreen divided vertically by a narrow strip.

The modern passenger and driver comforts provided by Willowbrook, Duple and Plaxton were augmented by the well-tried heavy duty specification adapted from the Bedford truck designs, an instance being the KM series 16 ton truck axles. These refinements obviously attracted a huge market, users including National (Shamrock and Rambler) and Barton.

YMT 1975 was the year when 466 cu. in. engines were replaced by Bedford's 500 cu. in. models and when the YMT chassis, receiving power from a 157 bhp design of the 500 engine, took over from the YRT version. Again a variety of operators and coach builders acquired YMT chassis to meet their requirements, including National Travel, Grey-Green, who favoured a Duple fifty-three seater vehicle, the National Coal Board with vehicles with Willowbrook bodywork, Plaxton, and, interestingly, Van Hool, whose Aragon design was ideal for touring purposes. An independent firm in Scotland, Fraser of Elgin, employed a Bedford YMT with Duple C53F body in 1979 and in 1980 Moss Motor Tours (Isle of Wight) purchased a Bedford YMT/Plaxton coach. Barton recently received two YMT/Plaxton C53F coaches, along with Smiths of Tysoe. In 1981–82 Newmans Coaches of New Zealand purchased YMT/Plaxton coaches.

JJL Production of the JJL midi-bus commenced in 1976, this being of semi-integral chass/body design powered by a 330 cu. in. diesel engine transversely mounted and having 16 in. wheels. With accommodation for twenty-seven sitting and ten standing, the JJL is valuable for city centre or rural routes.

YNT/YMQ The late 1970s and early 1980s brought some important developments in the Bedford coach and truck market. The year 1978 witnessed the production of the three millionth Bedford and the appearance of the YNT chassis with an 8.2 litre turbo-charged diesel engine, delivering 206 bhp at just 2,500 rpm; with a mid engine layout the Bedford YNT can be said to be one of the most powerful U.K. built coach chassis, displaying impressive road holding and stability.

In the early 1980s National (South Wales) was among several organisations introducing Bedford YMQ coaches with Duple bodies, in this case DP 45F and B 45F, and in 1981–82 United Counties received three Bedford YMQ chassis to carry Lex Vehicle Engineering bodies for use in Leighton Buzzard.

A Bedford YRQ 193 in. wheelbase coach carrying Duple Viceroy bodywork, 1970.

*A Smiths of Tysoe Bedford YMT featuring Plaxton
Supreme Coachwork.*

B.M.M.O.

The Birmingham and Midland Motor Omni-bus Company Limited (B.M.M.O.) dates back to 1905 but from the early 1920s to 1940 B.M.M.O. made their own bus and coach chassis near Smethwick. Pre 1945 examples of B.M.M.O. passenger vehicles include the SOSQL (1928), ON (1934), and the SOSIM of 1929 which was a forward control single deck chassis with either a B.M.M.O. 4.3 litre petrol or the company's six cylinder petrol model.

The last B.M.M.O. built buses, numbers 5930/37/53/77, were withdrawn from service in February 1981, and one of the final journeys was the R83 route from Rugby to Brownsover Estate.

Double Deckers

D5 In the war years B.M.M.O. purchased Daimler, A.E.C. and Leyland double deckers, but in 1949 the group launched the D5 double decker. This featured the company's 8 litre engine, hydraulic brakes and constant mesh gearbox, and a full length bonnet front which concealed the radiator. About half had a rear platform door.

D7/D9 Numerous routes in the Midland Red area were operated by the firm's B.M.M.O. D7 double decker powered by the company's 8 litre diesel engine while the gearbox was of the four speed constant mesh type, Metropolitan–Cammell supplying the bodywork. The D9 double decker appeared in 1958, measuring 8 ft. wide and 30 ft. long with a 17 ft. 1½ in. wheelbase, and powered by the B.M.M.O. 10.5 litre engine. The D9 stayed in production until 1966.

Single Deckers

S SERIES In 1936–39 B.M.M.O. tried out prototype 8 litre rear engined single deckers in co-operation with Metropolitan–Cammell, referring to these as the S5 series. In 1948 B.M.M.O. started to produce the S6, which was of similar design to their S5, although the width was increased from 7 ft. 6 in. to 8 ft. About three hundred and sixty buses of the S8, S9 and S10 range were built between 1947 and 1950, followed by the S11 and S12 in 1950. This underfloor engined single decker had an overall length of 29 ft. 3 in., accommodated forty-four seated passengers, and was powered by a B.M.M.O. 8.03 litre six cylinder oil engine positioned between the front and rear axles. B.M.M.O.'s S13 did not

Midland Red B.M.M.O. S21 on the X92 route.

have a separate cab, and the entrance was in front of the wheels, the weight being one ton lighter than the S12, but had similar dimensions. The S14 was revealed in 1954 as a bus of integral construction possessing a 16 ft. 4 in. wheelbase, four speed gearbox and independent front suspension together with disc brakes on all wheels, and accommodation for forty-four seated passengers. S15 underfloor engined single deckers boasted the B.M.M.O. 8.03 litre six cylinder engine, making their début in 1957 and remaining in production for some five years. Further single deckers included the S16 (1962), the S17 and the S21.

C1 AND C2 A total of fifty-seven express coaches were constructed between 1948 and 1950. The C1 sported a 27 ft. 6 in. long, 7 ft. 6 in. wide body, together with improved seating for thirty passengers embarking on express journeys. With the 8.03 litre B.M.M.O. six cylinder engine mounted in a horizontal position beneath the floor, the C1 was equipped with servo assisted hydraulic brakes, and C1 and C2 vehicles could be observed carrying Duple coachwork.

B.M.M.O. D9 Midland Red double decker.

BRISTOL

Bristol passenger vehicles before the Second World War included the B type single deck chassis (1926), the H and J types of 1933 and the Bristol K — a 7 ft. 6 in. wide single deck model with a 16 ft. 2 in. wheelbase. In 1937 Bristol launched the L chassis for single deck work as used by North Western Road Car Company and Eastern Counties, and during 1944 the K type bus re-appeared as the K5G with Gardner engines and K6A with A.E.C. 7.7 litre units, while other variations included the K6B employed by Rotherham, and Hampshire and Dorset.

BRISTOL L Similar to the earlier series, the 1946 Bristol L single deck chassis was powered by a variety of engines — Gardner 4LW or 5LW oil models or the A.E.C. six cylinder oil engine, while a Gardner 6LW model became available later. Chassis were named according to the engine

Bristol L5G/Eastern Coach Works in service with Eastern National, 1950.

they carried — L4Gs had Gardner 4LW units whilst L5G and L6A chassis received power from the 5LW and A.E.C. engines respectively, and the L6G was powered by the 6LW engine. Eastern Coach Works provided bodies for a larger number of the post war single deck L series including buses operated by Eastern National and Eastern Counties whose fleet featured L4G and L5G chassis, while instances of L6A models were in evidence with Crosville, and Wiltshire and Dorset ran L6B Bristols. L6G Bristol single deckers were powered by the Gardner 6LW engine as seen in the K series double deck range of Bristol buses.

BRISTOL LW The wider 8 ft. buses were designated LW5G and LW6B while vehicles which were both wider and longer than before received the titles of LWL5G and LWL6B, and were powered by Gardner and Bristol engines respectively. Manufactured between 1951 and 1954, buses in this series were supplied with five speed gearboxes and served with authorities such as

Bristol LS6G/Eastern Coach Works bus built in 1953 and owned by Royal Blue.

Thames Valley, Western National and United Counties, all of whom owned buses with Eastern Coach Works' bodies.

BRISTOL LS The LS appeared in 1950. Four models were available, known as LS4G, LS5G, LS6G, powered by Gardner 4HLW, 5HLW and 6HLW engines respectively, and the LS6B, powered by a Bristol AUW six cylinder engine. United and Durham and Southern National had LS5Gs with Eastern Coach Works' bodies, while London Transport experimented with a bus of the same chassis and body type, based at Reigate Garage before sending it back to the company. The turning circle was 59 ft. 2 in., and overall length 30 ft., while its suspension consisted of semi-elliptical leaf springs with Metalastik shackles shock absorbers on the front axle.

LL With a 19 ft. wheelbase and 7 ft. 6 in. width, the LL single decker made its début in 1950, engine types providing the various classifications — the LL5G featuring a Gardner 5LW engine, the LL6G coming with a 6LW unit from Gardner, while a Bristol six cylinder engine powered the LL6B vehicle. Crosville was one of several operators with LL6B/Eastern Coach Work buses while LL5Gs could also be seen with this company and with United Counties, Southern Vectis and West Yorkshire.

LH AND LHS Alexander was one of several companies providing coachwork for the Bristol LH chassis, while the short wheelbase Bristol

A United Counties Bristol MW6G with Eastern Coach Works body (above).

Bristol LL5G in service with West Yorkshire (1951) carrying Eastern Coach Works B39R body (right).

LHS was suitable for relatively short journeys such as those linking a city's stations, the model having a 24 ft. overall length and a 12 ft. 6 in. wheelbase and a width of 7 ft. $6\frac{1}{2}$ in., thus facilitating work in heavy traffic. London Transport operated seventeen Bristol LHS buses seating twenty-six people, having Eastern Coach Works bodies and a Leyland 0.401 six cylinder oil engine, on routes such as the C11 Holloway Service.

The more recent Bristol LHS is equipped with a Leyland 402 diesel engine. As a purpose designed 8.5/9.0 metre coach the LHS is ideal for

operators wanting a thirty-five seater coach with a 52 ft. turning circle and gross vehicle weight of 8.5 tons. The robust LHS frame allows a front entrance and mid mounted horizontal engine.

SC AND MW The single decker SC featured a 14 ft. $4\frac{1}{2}$ in. wheelbase and either Gardner or Perkins engines with again Eastern Coach Works bodies, whilst the Bristol MW, coming into service in 1957, two years after the SC, usually had the same coachwork. The MW's wheelbase measured 16 ft. 10 in. The MW5G was powered by a Gardner 5HLW engine, while a 6HLW was found in the MW6G range of single deckers as in the Thames Valley and United Counties fleets.

BRISTOL K, KS, KSW SERIES The K series was placed in production again towards the end of the Second World War, K5G being the designation of vehicles equipped with a Gardner engine, while those having an A.E.C. unit were referred to as K6A types. London Transport had about two hundred of these K buses on loan from the Tilling group because of the shortage of passenger vehicles after the war, and an external feature of the K5G's and K6A's was the London Transport badge mounted on the radiator. United and Durham District Services had among its fleet examples of the K6B powered by a Bristol 8.2 litre engine, whilst Maidstone and District, Western National, and Hampshire and Dorset also put K6As on the run.

With production of the K series ceasing in 1950, Bristol launched the KS chassis with similar dimensions. A 27 ft. long vehicle, most of the models had Eastern Coach Works' bodies, serving, for instance with Eastern Counties. Models with Bristol and Gardner engines were known as KS5B and KS5G vehicles. The move towards

Bristol SC4LK/Eastern Coach Works C33F with Crosville, 1960, powered by a Gardner 4LK (right).

London Transport Bristol LHS/Eastern Coach Works, acquired in the mid 1970s, seen on C11 Mini-bus service (below).

wider passenger vehicles was partly responsible for the KSW double deckers whose 8 ft. width was six inches greater than that of the KS model's. The various KSW models included KSW6B (Bristol engines), KSW6G (Gardner 6LW engines), and KSW5G (Gardner 5LW engines). It is interesting to note that all KSW buses were equipped with Eastern Coach Works' bodies, on the roads with authorities such as Bristol, Hampshire and Dorset United Counties and the Notts and Derby Traction Company.

LODEKKA LD SERIES During 1949 Bristol unveiled the prototype Lodekka bus LDX001. The following year witnessed the introduction of LDX002 and its distinctive chrome front bumper. These had a new design for the period, having chassis permitting normal highbridge bodywork, while the overall height was that of a standard lowbridge type double decker. Operators favoured the Bristol Lodekka with Eastern Coach Works bodies where the engine and radiator were at the front, and the gearbox straight behind. By offsetting the drive inside the gearbox the output shaft could be placed over to the offside close to the main chassis frame, so leaving space on the centre line for the gangway to be dropped into a well below the floor level of the seats.

Prototype LDX's featured a 15 ft. 11 in. wheelbase. LDs had 16 ft. 8½ in. wheelbases and a width of 8 ft. With Bristol AVW, Gardner 5LW or 6LW engines, they were referred to as LD6B, LD5G and LD6G respectively. The six pre-production Lodekkas had full length slatted radiator grilles, later followed by those of a full length mesh type and the smaller mesh grille. The bus company, Eastern Counties, had only LD5G models while United Counties and Eastern National favoured LD5Gs and the 6B designs. Other operators with LD Bristols included Hampshire and Dorset (ninety-nine vehicles) Wiltshire and Dorset (thirty-eight), Scottish Omnibuses (one hundred and fifty-two), Crosville (three hundred and fifty-one) and Bristol and Cheltenham who had about two hundred LDs in service.

A Notts and Derby Traction Company Bristol KSW6B/Eastern Coach Works double decker.

Bristol LD6B/Eastern Coach Works, in service with United Counties, equipped with a Bristol engine.

In 1957 seven LDs were built to an extended length of 30 ft. and were named LDLs in service with Hampshire and Dorset, Bristol Tramways, Western Nation, Thames Valley and Notts and Derby authorities, all equipped with 6G engines and either four or five speed gearboxes. Appearing during the late 1950s, the LDX003 and LDX004 prototype chassis had overall lengths of 27 ft. and 30 ft. respectively. LDS types had engine cowls without radiator grills when equipped with Cave–Browne–Cave heating systems. The only LD models acquired by Brighton Hove and District were of the LDS6B type.

LODEKKA FS AND FL SERIES

LODEKKA FS AND FL SERIES Bristol production models were released in 1960 having similar appearance to the LD marque except that the sunken gangway downstairs was avoided by restricting the depth of the main chassis side members and strengthening the trusses formed by the body side members. From 1960 the 27 ft. model (with its 16 ft. $11\frac{1}{4}$ in. wheelbase) was entitled the FS model (F:Flat floor; S:Short), and the 30 ft. chassis (19 ft. $2\frac{1}{4}$ in. wheelbase) was designated FL (L:Long). Engine types provided the designations' suffixes, leading to a series of Lodekkas known as FSF6G, FSF6L, FLF6G, and FLF6L, all coming with Eastern Coach Works bodies.

The FS series generally had manually operated platform doors, although some had no doors. The

A Leyland 0.600-powered Bristol FLF6L/Eastern Coach Works vehicle, built in 1967 for Hants and Dorset, currently owned by a Stockport school (left).

Alexander bodied Bristol VRT built in 1977 for Tayside Regional Council (below).

success of FS and FL Lodekka passenger vehicles is reflected in the large numbers purchased, especially by Red and White who had twenty-five FS and twenty FL models, one FL staying in service until 1980, and Eastern Counties and West Yorkshire received one hundred and twenty and one hundred and fifty-five respectively, while Crosville acquired about one hundred and thirty FS models; in fact, Crosville still had a 1964 FS6G in service in 1981 (registration GFM 196C).

OTHER BRISTOL VEHICLES The VRT models can be observed in service with many companies such as Maidstone and District, South Wales, and Lincoln who acquired VRTLLs in the early 1980s with Gardner 6LXB engines. Rhymney Valley received VRT84s in 1980 while, at the same time, East Midlands purchased some with Gardner 6LXB engines. In 1980 Tayside withdrew their VRTLL3s after years of faithful service, at the same time giving a Bristol VRT199 a new lease of life by converting it to a single door

A Western Scottish Bristol REMH with Alexander body, delivered in 1971.

Unusual Pennine B34D bodywork on a Reading Corporation Bristol RELL6G, built in 1968.

model with coach seating for use on private hires. London County acquired fifteen Bristol VRTs in 1977 but in the space of four years all were sold to Bristol Omnibus Company for their use. Double deck Bristol VRTs may be seen with Ribble, Tayside Regional Council and Crosville.

Bristol RE buses can be observed with Ipswich Borough Transport and Eastern Counties, and Western Scottish boasts REMH vehicles. However, in the early 1980s Colchester withdrew two RELL6L buses, and in 1981 Alder Valley sold a dozen RELL6Gs with Eastern Coach Works bodies to Eastern Counties, while City Bus, Northern Ireland, received an ex-United RELL6G with Eastern Coach Work body in 1981. Until recently, Reading Corporation operated Bristol RELL6G single deckers with unusual Pennine B34D bodywork.

B.U.T.

The company of British United Traction Ltd (B.U.T.) came about when A.E.C. and Leyland combined to make and sell trolleybuses in the mid 1940s. In 1921 A.E.C. had a test track for trolleybuses at Southall. At that time bus chassis were employed, their petrol engines replaced by electric-drive — in fact, A.E.C.'s first trolleybus was based on the S-type bus. Following the Second World War, there seemed to be a liking for three axled trolleybuses and B.U.T. produced two and three axle models. The new firm initially manufactured trolleybuses at Leyland's premises at Kingston-on-Thames, moving production in 1948 to A.E.C.'s Southall plant and the Lancashire factory at Leyland, but some vehicles were made at Crossley Works, Errwood Park near Stockport and at Scammell's Watford factory.

B.U.T. 9641T Making an appearance in 1946, this three axled trolleybus had an 18 ft. 5 in. wheelbase and could carry 7 ft. 6 in. or 8 ft. wide single or double deck bodywork. Crompton Parkinson, Metro-Vickers, G.E.C., B.T.H. or English Electric power plants were available. Remaining in production until June 1958, the 9641T saw service with authorities such as Newcastle, Nottingham, Bournemouth and Cardiff, with coachbuilders including Brush, Weymann and Metropolitan-Cammell.

B.U.T. 9611T, 9612T In keeping with the 9641T, the 9611T made its début in 1947 with a choice of five types of motor. A two axle trolleybus with a 16 ft. 4. in wheelbase, it proved popular and was found with Bradford Corporation (the last operator of trolleybuses in Britain), Nottingham, and Brighton Corporation who favoured Weymann H56R bodied vehicles. Featuring a front positioned contractor gear, the 9611T had a seating capacity of fifty-six. Modernised and referred to as the 9612T in 1951, it stayed in production until 1957. The 9612T served in places such as Ashton-under-Lyne and Manchester, the latter Corporation's 9612T having Burlingham H60R coachwork.

B.U.T. 9613T Glasgow Corporation acquired examples of the 9613T trolleybus, which came on the market in 1956. The 9613T was a two axle double deck vehicle designed to take 30 ft. long

B.U.T. 9612T/Burlingham, 1955, seen with Manchester Corporation livery.

bodywork whose width was only 8 ft. on its 18 ft. 6 in. wheelbase, extended by one inch in 1957. During the following year an alternative 16 ft. 4 in. wheelbase was offered as an option. A selection of motors was offered. B.U.T. continued production until 1963.

B.U.T. 9642T To compensate for the cessation of production of the 9641T, B.U.T. launched the 9642T in 1957 as a three axle double decker coming in 7 ft. 6 in. or 8 ft. widths. Manufacture continued until 1963.

B.U.T. ETB/1 In an effort to gain a foothold in the single deck trolleybus market, B.U.T. introduced during 1950 a two axle single deck chassis designated RETB/1 and LETB/1, for the right hand drive and left hand drive versions respectively. However, only twenty-one saw service on domestic routes, all with Glasgow Corporation.

Coming with a rear or side mounted contractor motor, the ETB/1 accommodated five varieties of motors and was at first 33 ft. long with a 17 ft. 6 in. wheelbase, but 15 ft. 7 in. and 18 ft. 6 in. wheelbases were offered as options in 1951. In 1958 the last ETB/1 was received by Glasgow, but manufacturing for overseas markets carried on until the mid 1960s.

COMMER

Commer passenger vehicles were in evidence before 1945 in the form of the 1931 Centaur, the PN3 of 1935 and the PNF4 with its 13 ft. 9 in. wheelbase and Commer engine.

COMMANDO In June 1946 the Commer Commando Q4 entered the passenger vehicle market capable of carrying twenty-eight or thirty-two people on its 15 ft. 9 in. wheelbase. It was powered by the pre-war Commer 4.08 litre petrol engine, coupled to a four speed crash gearbox. A $1\frac{1}{2}$ deck layout was employed by the R.A.F. and a number of air lines including B.O.A.C., whose twenty seat coach had a large luggage compartment under the upper deck or observation saloon;

these buses carried Park Royal bodywork, and were employed for the transportation of air passengers. David MacBrayne's fleet in Scotland acquired seven Commer Commandos with Croft bodywork, their fleet numbers being 69 to 74 and 99, all of which were licensed in mid 1948.

AVENGER The forward control Avenger appeared in 1948, its new 4.75 litre petrol engine being unusual in that it was mounted low down with the cylinders tilted at an angle of 70 degrees

Commer Commando seen on a tilt test before delivery to B.O.A.C. in the late 1940s.

Commer twenty-five seater, 1953 (top left).

A Lisbon based Commer displaying interesting interior and bodywork features (bottom left).

to the vertical so permitting it to be positioned low under the cab floor — thus obviating the need for a bonnet in the middle and consequently permitting two passengers to occupy the area alongside the driver. Operators with the Avenger included Maidstone and District, bodywork coming from firms such as Harrington, Plaxton and Yeates. The vehicle remained in production from 1949 until 1952.

OTHER VEHICLES 1952 a chassis-less version of the Avenger, the Contender, appeared. A light alloy vehicle incorporating the Commer transmission, axles, engine and gearbox plus Harrington bodywork, with the choice of a front or central entrance, the Contender had a 30 ft. overall length, 8 ft. width and an unladen weight of only 4 tons 12 cwt. The T355 twenty-five seater was a popular bus for operation in the 1950s, this vehicle featuring a sliding passengers' door.

COMMER BUSES OVERSEAS The value of Commer passenger vehicles was underlined by the international interest shown in them. The Superpoise, with bodywork from local firms, was operated in Natal, the Netherlands, and British Guiana (now Guyana). Thailand, North Borneo, the Faeroe Isles and Lisbon, Portugal were other foreign markets which bought Commer passenger vehicles.

CROSSLEY

Crossley Motors was formed from the Crossley Brothers gas and oil engine manufacturers in 1910, during the First World War becoming a major supplier of military vehicles to the Royal Flying Corps. In 1928 the Crossley Eagle chassis was revealed as the firm's first full-size PSV product from its Manchester factory. Buses prior to 1945 included the Type 8, the Mancunian (1930), and the Crossley Condor (1930), a double deck chassis with a 16 ft. 7½ in. wheelbase. In 1950 A.E.C. purchased the share capital. One of the last large orders for Crossley was the delivery of two hundred and sixty buses to Birmingham with Crossley bodies, and the last Crossley was finished in 1953. The only Crossley Regent built was 434 BTE, built in 1957 for Darwen Corporation, this coming about before A.E.C. disposed of the Crossley name.

Double Deckers

DD42 SERIES A prototype double decker was built during the war, entering service with Manchester Corporation in 1943. The first post war buses were of the DD42/3 variety, the DD42/2 model never going into production. The standard DD42 chassis was offered with a Crossley 8.6 litre six cylinder direct injection engine of a type different from pre-war makes. A typical post 1945 Crossley bus was the DD42/4, the first 8 ft. wide model of this make to be delivered entering service with Manchester in 1947.

Examples of the DD42/5 could be seen with Eastbourne Corporation whose fifty-six seaters

A Crossley DD42/7 with Crossley bodywork, delivered to Liverpool Corporation in 1949.

had East Lancashire bodywork. During 1948 Crossley launched the DD42/7 as a 7 ft. 6 in. wide double decker with 16 ft. 7½ in. wheelbase, Crossley 8.6 litre engine and triple servo brakes as standard. Portsmouth Corporation, Liverpool and Birmingham were examples of operators owning the DD42/7 which offered a choice of transmission — a four speed synchromesh gearbox, four speed constant mesh gearbox, or an automatic system with Brockhouse turbo transmitter.

The DD42/8 entered service in 1948 with authorities such as Oldham, Derby and Manchester, initially boasting a 16 ft. 7½ in. wheelbase, lengthened in 1950 to accommodate 27 ft. long bodies, the width being 8 ft. and employing Crossley's own six cylinder 8.6 litre direct injection oil engine.

Examples of Single Deckers

SD42 SERIES Just as the war finished Crossley was asked to supply almost two thousand single deckers for the Netherlands, including about five hundred SD42/1 forty-eight seat buses and over

A Crossley Dominion TDD64 trolleybus with Manchester Corporation, 1950.

four hundred SD42/2 thirty-eight seaters. During 1948 the success of the SD42 series was further highlighted by the advent of the SD42/6 model with a 17 ft. 7 in. wheelbase and width of 7 ft. 6 in. and powered by a Crossley six cylinder 8.6 litre direct injection oil engine. The following year a 42/7 version was introduced, which had a choice of either a four or five speed constant mesh or synchromesh gearbox. This version stayed in production until 1951.

Examples of Crossley Trolley buses

The Crossley Dominion TDD64 made its début in 1950 as a double deck trolleybus of the three axle design, 30 ft. long with a width of 7 ft. 6 in. or 8 ft. and provided with Metro–Vickers motors. Crossley Empire TDD42s were two axle double deck trolleybuses accommodating a body length of 26 ft., either 7 ft. 6 in. or 8 ft. in width, and served in areas such as Ashton-under-Lyne, Walsall and Manchester.

DAIMLER

The Daimler Motor Syndicate in the U.K. began in the late 1800s, taking its name from Gottlieb Daimler, and, towards the end of the century, the Daimler Motor Company was established in Coventry, producing a variety of vehicles. During the 1900s Daimler manufactured buses, employing A.E.C. and Gardner diesel engines and the Daimler pre-selective gearbox, while during the Second World War the COG5 buses (the designation signifying commercial, oil engined, Gardner, five cylinder) were popular, later known as CWGs ('W' referring to wartime production).

CV SERIES Following the war, the former CWD6 became the CVD6, the 'V' standing for victory. This Victory series chassis was introduced in 1946 with a choice of four engines — Daimler CD6 8.4 litre, A.E.C. 7.7 litre or Gardner 5LW and 6LW models, the chassis referred to as CVD6, CVA6, CVG5 and CVG6 respectively,

but the A.E.C. engine was withdrawn during 1947. In 1953 a 27 ft. long body was supplied for the 16 ft. 4 in. wheelbase. Original CV type buses were equipped with vacuum brakes but in 1956 air brakes were optional and in the same year an 18 ft. 6 in. wheelbase chassis came on the scene — CVD30 and CVG30, according to whether it had Daimler or Gardner engines. From 1947 onwards Daimler started making single deck buses in addition to double deck versions with a number of operators showing an interest in the CV-SD type of single deck vehicle, among whom were Exeter Corporation and West Bromwich Corporation whose CVG5 single deckers carried Metropolitan–Cammell bodywork. It is interesting to note that the often forgotten Associated Coachbuilders (A.C.B.) of Sunderland provided bodywork for a number of double deck

A Daimler CVD6 with Northern Counties coachwork, built in 1948 for Liverpool Corporation.

A Salford Corporation CVG6, built in 1962 with Metropolitan-Cammell bodywork.

CVG5 vehicles for Sunderland Corporation in 1954, with A.C.B. employing a new type of bonnet. These Daimler CVG5/ACB buses accommodated thirty-three upstairs and twenty-five on the lower deck. The manufacture of the CV series ended in the mid 1960s during which time numerous transport authorities had found the chassis to be of value: Birmingham, Liverpool and Coventry were examples of areas with CVA6 buses, while CVD6's could be found in Colches-ter, Cleethorpes, and with SHMD; Lancaster had CVG5 buses while CVG6s were operated by Salford, Aberdeen, West Bromwich and Belfast.

LONGER CV BUSES In 1956 Daimler took advantage of amended regulations concerning vehicle lengths and introduced a longer version of the CVG6 bus to the public — the CVG6–30 with an 18 ft. 6 in. wheelbase rather than 16 ft. 4 in. With Daimler engines, these chassis were called CVD650–30, and the Gardner engined model was referred to as the CVG6LX–30. Different bodywork designs were available; thus,

Glasgow's CVD650–30 buses had Alexander Coachwork while Leeds' CVG6LX–30 vehicles came with Roe bodies and Leon Motor Services of Finningley favoured the seventy-three seater Roe CVD650–30 vehicle while Willowbrook also supplied bodywork for CVG6–30 chassis.

CV S/D Only a small quantity of Daimler CVD650–220 and CVG6–200 single deckers were made, mostly for export in the late 1950s, having a 22 ft. wheelbase. The Daimler CV series single deck chassis had a 17 ft. $2\frac{1}{2}$ in. wheelbase and either a Daimler CD6 8.4 litre or Gardner 5LW oil engine, being named CVD6 or CVG6 respectively. A variety of body manufacturers provided coachwork, including Burlingham, Duple, Metropolitan Cammell, and Park Royal. Single deck CVD6 vehicles also had coachwork by Associated Coachbuilders, with Exeter Corporation Transport and Smiths Eagle Coachways being examples of operators using CVD6 buses.

CD SERIES In 1948, whilst still producing the CVG6, Daimler launched the CD series, and the large fluted radiator of the CD650 made it easily recognizable. Based on the CVD6, but coming with a 10.6 litre Daimler engine, the CD had several interesting features, including the first power assisted brakes. Daimler felt sure this double deck chassis with 16 ft. 4 in. wheelbase, fifty-six seats and 150 bhp engine would prove exceptionally popular on the domestic market. In fact, only a dozen or so CD650s served in the U.K., for instance, with the Blue Bus Service in Derbyshire, the 20 ft. single deck CD650 proving more popular abroad than in the U.K.

CS/CC SERIES Among a number of alterations in design and technical specifications introduced by Daimler in the mid 1950s, a notable one was the front end and bonnet, restyled in fibre glass and named the 'Manchester front'. In 1958 Daimler offered customers a manual gearbox, the CSD6, CSG5 and CSG6 models being equipped with David Brown four speed gearboxes, but only about forty were delivered, CSG6s to Cardiff,

Daimler CVA6 with Weymann bodywork delivered to Liverpool Corporation in 1949.

New to Bolton Transport in 1960, this CVG6-30 served S.E.L.N.E.C. (Northern) in 1969–73 (left).

A Daimler CCG6 with Roe bodywork, built in the 1960s for South Shields.

A Daimler CRG6LXR/Roe, built in 1976 (right).

SHMD and South Shields, and CSG5 buses to Burton and Grimsby. These models were super-seded by the constant mesh gearbox, CCG5 and CCG6 models of 1963.

The CCG chassis was of a forward control design with air operated or triple servo vacuum brakes and a 16 ft. 4 in. wheelbase. In the early 1960s Jaguar had acquired Guy and Daimler and the gearbox for this series was a Guy four speed

constant mesh unit. Those with Gardner 5LW engines were termed CCG5 while 6LW oil engined chassis were designated CCG6. About one hundred CCG buses were constructed by 1968 when production stopped. Roe H63R bodied CCG6 buses were in evidence with South Shields Corporation Transport, while Chesterfield owned some with Weymann bodies, and Burton acquired examples of CCG5 buses. In January 1981 the last double decker to run in Darlington was a Daimler CCG5.

CL SERIES The CL series was a lighter version of the CV chassis and prospective buyers saw it at Earls Court Commercial Motor Show in 1952 with a Birmingham front, 10 cwt. lighter than the CVG5. Powered by a Gardner 5LW oil engine the CLG5 came with a pre-selector gearbox and fluid flywheel and remained in production for three years, many of its weight saving qualities becoming available in the CV versions of Daimler buses.

Rear Engined Daimlers

FLEETLINE The CRG6-30 or 'Fleetline' RE30 rear engined double deck bus was introduced in September 1960. It had a short 16 ft. 3 in. wheelbase, 30 ft. overall length, and a height of 13 ft. 4 in., and seated up to seventy-eight passengers. Early versions were equipped with Daimler CD6 engines but production models were powered by a 10.5 litre Gardner 6LX mounted at the rear; the 8.4 6LW engine was also a further option. CRG6LW models could be found with SHMD and the Ayrshire company of A1 Service. One advantage which the Fleetline had over rival Atlanteans was a central gangway on lower and upper decks, while the wide entrance in front of the axle was only about one foot above street level, thus facilitating easy entry and exit. The design

Owned by S.H.M.D. this Daimler CRG6LW features Northern Counties bodywork.

of axle and transmission allowed for a low, flat floor, and in the mid 1960s the SRG6-33 chassis could accommodate a 33 ft. long bus with room for up to eighty-six seats.

Operators saw the value of this impressive bus with its large seating capacity and soon many fleets had Daimler rear engined passenger vehicles. These varied in design depending on specifications required by the customer. Some preferred shorter chassis than those offered as standard; SHMD and Walsall were examples of this sort of client, the Walsall models carrying sixty-five passengers on CRG6-27 chassis. The CRG6LX-33 double deckers and SRG6LX-33 and SRG6LX-36 single deckers proved to be popular with transport authorities such as West Bromwich, Middlesbrough, Birkenhead, Midland Red and Glasgow.

The end of the 1960s witnessed the merger of Daimler with Leyland, whose Atlanteans were already in a strong position on the bus market, and soon a Leyland 680 engine was employed by Daimler, the chassis being referred to as CRL6, the start of a renaming period of Daimler chassis. However, the end of the 1970s saw Daimler's name disappear on new models, to be replaced by Leyland Fleetline insignia. Today there are still examples of Daimler Fleetlines. In 1981, for example, Chester rebuilt Fleetline number 48, while others have changed hands, the early 1980s witnessing Southdown Daimler Fleetlines 2124-6 going to East Kent and Wrexham (Crosville) and

A London Transport DMS Daimler displaying separate entrance and exit points.

some 1965 Western vehicles being acquired by Alexander (Northern). Other authorities, however, have withdrawn Fleetlines. Leeds in mid 1981 took out of service models with Roe bodies, while in Cardiff a Daimler Fleetline recently employed for driver training became an office bus.

LONDON'S DMS VEHICLES

London Transport was impressed by the Daimler Fleetline and the initial order for seventeen buses saw them on London streets in 1971, the authority purchasing DMS vehicles until 1978. DMS vehicles were Daimler Fleetline one man operated buses with a capacity for eighty-nine people — forty-four sitting upstairs, twenty-four sitting downstairs and twenty-one standing. Engines were Gardner 6LXB 10.45 litre or Leyland 0.680 11.1 litre with bodywork from Metropolitan–Cammell–Weymann and Park Royal. The livery of London's DMS vehicles has been altered during production, two hundred and fifty being given an exterior white band between lower and upper saloons while entrance doors were coloured yellow to emphasize the point of entry. Introduced in 1974, London's DM buses were Daimler Fleetline crew operated vehicles taking seventy-six passengers — forty-four sitting on the top deck, twenty-seven on the lower deck and five standing — with the same engines as DMS buses.

The DMO is a Daimler Fleetline with removable roof, employed for sightseeing purposes, carrying forty-three people upstairs, thirty-one downstairs, and, as a one man operated bus, it has a combined front entrance and exit. Introduced in 1977 to London, the DMO is powered by a Gardner 6LX 10.45 litre engine and measures 9.35 metres in length, 2.50 metres in width and has an unladen height of 4.25 metres.

It is worth noting that London Transport began selling large numbers of comparatively new DMS buses in the late 1970s and early 1980s, and some would argue that there were numerous reasons for those sales: bodywork repair was difficult because rivet holes were not always standard, the bus was heavier than rival designs, while airlocks in fuel systems were common. A firm in Essex, Ensign, has bought about five hundred London DMS buses and re-designed them, providing, for example, single front entrance doors, the final product being sold to a number of operators in

areas of Oxford, East Anglia and Bishop Auckland, and to Chesterfield and Lancashire United Transport.

ROADLINER The 1964 Earls Court Show introduced the public to the Roadliner, powered by either a Cummins 9.6 litre or Perkins 8.36 litre engine; the model was referred to as SRP8 with an 18 ft. 6 in. wheelbase and SRC6 with the Cummins engine. Many Roadliners saw service abroad in places such as South Africa, Canada and Australia, and comparatively few SRC6 buses were in evidence on domestic roads, though some were found in Darlington and with private operators.

FREELINE The D650HS was an underfloor engined single deck chassis which Daimler announced in 1951, having been tried and tested from 1949, finally appearing with either a 16 ft. 4 in. or 17 ft. 6 in. wheelbase for 30 ft. or 32 ft. overall length, and 7 ft. 6 in. or 8 ft. widths. Given the designation 'Freeline' two models were available — the D650HS and the G6HS with Daimler's 10.6 litre and Gardner's 8.4 litre engines respectively. In 1954 a 20 ft. 4 in. wheelbase Freeline was introduced for use abroad. During 1965 the production of the CD650 horizontal and vertical engine stopped, but Daimler chassis designed for this unit could still carry the Gardner 10.5 litre 6LX or 6HLX, or the former 6LW or 6LHW engines. In 1951 hydraulic servo type brakes were used on the Freelines, these being replaced by air brakes in 1954. Most Freelines were sent abroad, chiefly to South Africa and New Zealand, and when manufacture of D650HS types was discontinued in 1964 under one hundred Freelines had been purchased for use in Britain.

Trolleybuses

Pre 1945 Daimler trolleybuses included those in service with West Hartlepool and following the war Daimler trolleybuses were seen in Glasgow and Rotherham, whose single deck models could accommodate thirty-eight passengers. In the mid 1950s Rotherham acquired a batch of double deck Daimler trolleybuses which stayed in use until the demise of trolleybuses in the area some ten years later.

DENNIS

Dennis of Guildford have been associated with a number of products including bicycles, fire appliances and trucks, their first passenger vehicle coming on the scene in 1905. Before 1945 the range of passenger vehicles included E types with dropped frame chassis, the F series in 1927, followed by the G and H series, this last type being Dennis' first forward control double deck vehicle. In the 1930s Dennis produced passenger vehicles such as the Dart, Lance I, Lancet I and II, the Lancet of 1936 together with the Falcon — the last new bus Dennis made before the war. Today, Hestair Dennis supply an interesting assortment of buses to operators in the U.K. and abroad.

Single Deckers

LANCETS The J3 was introduced at the end of 1945 as a single deck chassis of the forward control type featuring the Lancet II radiator. It was powered by a Dennis 7.9 litre oil engine. Those with Gardner 5LW units were referred to

as J4 types. Examples of bus companies with J3 and J4 vehicles included Aldershot and District, Yorkshire Traction Company, and East Kent, whose models had Park Royal bodies. Five years after the début of J3 vehicles, Dennis brought out the Lancet J10 which was, in fact, a 30 ft. long version of the J3, with variations such as the J10A and J10C. The J10 also proved to be a popular single decker for Aldershot and District (who also favoured the Lancet IV), along with companies such as East Kent: The Lancet IV was offered to the operators in 1952 as an underfloor engined single decker chassis with a wheelbase measuring 16 ft. 4 in. and featured a Dennis six cylinder engine plus five speed gearbox.

OTHER SINGLE DECKERS The pre-war Falcon reappeared in 1948 with a 16 ft. 6 in. wheelbase and a variety of engine choices, including

A Dennis Lancet II with Park Royal bodywork, built in the late 1930s for East Kent.

Perkins, Gardner and Dennis units. Bodywork was frequently supplied by Dennis, such as for Falcons in service with Southdown and East Kent. Dennis bodywork may also be witnessed on a single deck Pax V Dennis chassis (9390–2328) built in 1968 and currently in service with Abercony U.D.C. The early 1950s saw the advent of a number of Dennis single deck passenger vehicles on the market, such as the 1950 Dominant, whose frame was straight apart for small humps over the axles and over the engine, specifications including a Hobbs semi-automatic transmission and an underfloor engine. Only two Dominant buses were constructed before the Lancet UF was introduced. This bus possessed a 16 ft. 4 in. instead of 16 ft. 9 in. wheelbase, and the humps in the Dominant chassis were eliminated by building the Lancet UF frame 3 in. higher than before.

A new lightweight underfloor engined chassis named the Pelican appeared towards the end of 1954. Like the Lancet UF, this bus was designed in such a way that the driver's sitting position was lower than that of the passengers, while the 1954 Triton was built on a goods chassis adapted for passenger work.

Double Deckers

LANCE III The pre-war double deck Lance came back on the bus market in 1946 under the title of Lance III or K3, featuring a larger radiator, a 16 ft. $3\frac{1}{4}$ in. wheelbase, and a Dennis 7.6 litre engine. Vehicles with Gardner 5LW engines had the name of K4, and on these the radiator was concealed. The K4 could be seen with a number of companies such as Aldershot and District.

LOLINE During the early 1950s the Bristol Lodekka made an impact on the passenger vehicle market but was restricted to the nationalised Tilling and Scottish groups of companies. After

A 1968 bus with Dennis chassis and bodywork, originally owned by Llandudno U.D.C. and now with Aberconwy U.D.C., seen in Llandudno (right).

This Yeates bodied Dennis Lancet J3, negotiating a roundabout, was built in 1947 and was owned by Gash and Sons of Nottinghamshire (below).

negotiations, Dennis were granted permission to manufacture a Lodekka at Guildford with the name of Loline, for sale to any operator. In 1956 the first chassis with an 18 ft. 6 in. wheelbase and overall length of 30 ft. was completed. Designed to have a rear entrance and powered by a Gardner 6LW engine, this Loline I featured a five speed constant mesh overdrive gearbox. In 1958 the Loline II was unveiled with a 19 ft. wheelbase and provision for a front entrance if required, while two years later an optional 16 ft. $8\frac{1}{2}$ in. wheelbase was offered; in order to give strength in the front entrance area the two principal side members of the Loline II chassis were positioned farther apart than on the Loline I. Loline Is could be seen with Middlesbrough Corporation (Northern Counties bodywork) and Aldershot and District (East Lancashire bodies), while Loline IIs were common sights with North Western Road Car Company (East Lancashire Bodywork), Reading Corporation, Walsall Corporation, Barton and many other operators. Some Lolines had their livery changed when re-organisations took place — North Western buses with Alexander bodywork were repainted green after passing to Crosville, while Weymann bodied Loline IIIs originally supplied to Aldershot and District were later given Alder Valley livery.

The Loline III came on the scene in 1960 with wheelbases of 19 ft. $2\frac{1}{4}$ in., 16 ft. $11\frac{1}{4}$ in. and 18 ft.. A different style of radiator grille typified the Mark III, while air suspension for the rear wheels proved a popular improvement over earlier marques in the series. Buyers could choose between Gardner 6LX, 6LW or Leyland oil engines. Loline III production ended in 1967. Loline III models were in evidence with groups such as North Western, Aldershot and District, Leigh Corporation (who favoured the rear entrance over the more conventional one at the front) and Alder Valley, who still had Loline III's in service in the early 1980s.

JUBILANT The first of a new type Dennis chassis came on the market in 1977. A vertical front engined chassis, featuring air brakes, power

An Aldershot and District Dennis Loline/Alexander, built in 1961.

assisted steering and Gardner 6LXB engine, it is ideal for double or single deck buses. The Jubilant is in service in Hong Kong and Capetown and the front mounted engine drives to a straight rear axle via the Voith D851 transmission.

DOMINATOR The Dennis Dominator was constructed in 1977 with East Lancashire coachwork, this bodybuilder being the first to be associated with the Dominator chassis. The first Dominator was demonstrated with South Yorkshire P.T.E., but Leicester City Transport had

A South Yorkshire Transport Dennis Dominator received in 1981, carrying Alexander 'R' coachwork.

the first to enter service, and recently this organization possessed about seventy Dominators with Marshall and East Lancashire bodywork. The Dominator chassis is offered with either a 16 ft. 3 in. or 18 ft. 6 in. wheelbase and customers choose between a Rolls-Royce Eagle six cylinder oil engine or the Gardner 6LXB unit, but fully automatic Voith transmission is standard.

Most of the chassis is made at the Dennis Guildford factory, although side members come from elsewhere, and the company's leaf suspension ensures an excellent ride. Operators with Dominators include Eastbourne, Brighton and Manchester, whose vehicles have Maxwell gearboxes, while 1982–83 saw Chester receiving six

Dominators with Northern Counties bodies. The first of one hundred and seventy-four for South Yorkshire was received in May 1981, the rest coming in the 1982–84 period equipped with Rolls-Royce Eagle 220 engines and Alexander R type bodies. Perhaps versatility is part of Dennis' success with the Dominator range, in that a variety of engines may be fitted to the vehicle, while the single deck and double deck versions offer a wider choice for operators, Hartlepool, for instance, receiving half a dozen forty-three seat dual door single deckers with East Lancashire bodywork, whilst Darlington Corporation favours the single deck model with Marshall coachwork.

FALCON AND LANCETS When withdrawn from production, the Bristol RE left a niche for the Dennis Falcon H, a low floor, rear engined single decker powered by a horizontal Gardner engine. Initially titled Falcon I, the title was altered to Falcon H to denote a horizontal engine. The Falcon V (vertical engine) is suitable for double deck work, coming with a Mercedes-Benz V6 OM421 or a Perkins V8.640 unit, the

A Marshall bodied single deck Dennis Dominator, delivered to Darlington in 1980.

front part of the frame being similar to the Dominator, although somewhat higher, allowing bodywork to be built straight on the frame. Some authorities showing an interest in Falcons include Nottingham and Greater Manchester P.T.E. who are impressed by the many features, including the flat interior floor, while Leicester's Falcon H has a Duple Dominant fifty-one seat body with lighting by four tubes in the roof and an engine hatch with similar appearance to the Bristol RE in that it has a double cover.

The Lancet is a high floor, underfloor engine coach/bus chassis capable of taking Perkins or Leyland engines, exhibiting a radiator placed straight in front of the engine together with a choice of gearboxes. Examples of authorities with the Lancet include Portsmouth, Leicester, Tillingbourne Bus, and Blackpool, this last town receiving vehicles in 1982–83 with Perkins V8.540 engines and Marshall bodies.

DODGE

Dodge passenger vehicles before the war included the UF30A with an 11 ft. 4 in. wheelbase. In 1950 the 86/P6 bus chassis was promoted abroad, specifications including a Perkins P6 engine, and a 15 ft. 10 in. wheelbase, which was later lengthened to 16 ft. 2 in. In 1962 Dodge Brothers of Kew brought out a new forty-two seater forward entry bus with a straight main frame, powered by a Leyland 0.370 diesel engine, mounted vertically alongside the driver. During the late 1970s a battery powered passenger vehicle was tested.

Battery powered Dodge long wheelbase P.S.V.

FODEN

The name Foden is associated with a number of vehicles such as trucks and army transporters and it is with some surprise that people find that this Cheshire firm also manufactured buses and coaches, the first passenger vehicle being a 1914 steam bus built on a three-ton chassis. In the early 1930s Foden launched their first oil engined chassis for use with passenger vehicles. This was based on a Foden truck frame, having accommodation for twenty-six passengers, but, realising the potential of bus/coach chassis, Foden brought out the SDG chassis for single deck coachwork.

By now bodybuilders were showing an interest in the Foden expansion into passenger vehicles and Burlingham supplied the body for a thirty-two seater coach based on the SDG chassis. Specifications for the coach included a Gardner oil engine, Foden gearbox and an aluminium shell constructed specifically for it. The DDG6 double deck chassis with Burlingham bodywork followed.

A Warrington Corporation Foden PVD6/East Lancashire Coachworks H58R, seen on the Great Sankey route.

PVD In keeping with other passenger vehicle manufacturers, Foden saw the need for new buses after the Second World War, in 1945 announcing the PVD double decker which had a full width bonnet and concealed radiator giving a 'modern' appearance. The PVD had a 16 ft. 3 in. wheelbase and customers could choose between Gardner 5LW or 6LW engines, the chassis types so equipped being referred to as PVD5 and PVD6 respectively. In 1949 Foden introduced the company's FE6 engine, with a 4.09 litre capacity, to the PVD chassis but only one double decker was equipped with this unit.

Brakes for the PVD buses were hydaulic. The robust chassis included a cruciform crosspiece providing additional strength, a feature which added to the vehicle's potential. Operators who used PVD buses included PMT, who owned PVD6 models with Massey bodywork, and Warrington Corporation, whose fleet included PVD6 buses with Crossley and East Lancashire body-

work. In spite of the modern appearance and strong chassis, only about sixty PVD series buses were manufactured before production ceased in 1956.

PVSC AND PVFE Introduced in 1946, and manufactured concurrently with the PVD double deck chassis, the PVSC single deck chassis had a 17 ft. 6 in. wheelbase, with a choice of 7 ft. 6 in. or 8 ft. widths. A number of fleet owners acquired this chassis, including Bullock, the coach firm of Cheadle, the Green Bus Company in Staffordshire and Crown Coaches of Birtley, whose two PVSC6 vehicles had Associated Coachbuilders bodywork. The title PVSC6 was given to chassis with Gardner 6LW oil engines. The title became PVSC5 for models powered by the Gardner 5LW unit,

The famous Foden Band used this Foden PVR in the 1950s to travel to competitions.

A 1973 Foden single decker destined for work in Kingston, Jamaica.

although this engine was replaced totally by the six cylinder model in 1948.

Encouraged by their success with a Foden two stroke engine, the company introduced the FE6 unit to the PVSC series in 1949, consequently altering the designation of such chassis to PVFE. This chassis also featured a modified braking system in which a hydraulic attachment allowed oil to be circulated at a pressure of 1,000–1,200 psi; when pressure was applied to the brake, proportionate amounts of pressure were bled to set off the ordinary hydraulic master cylinder with some force. Fifty-two PVFE6 buses were manufactured between 1949 and 1950 when the PVRF series superseded it.

PVR SERIES The PVR was a single deck rear engined chassis coming with a 16 ft. wheelbase for domestic users and 19 ft. 6 in. for overseas buyers. A choice was given between a Gardner 6LW or a Foden FD6 two stroke oil engine, the titles of chassis being PVRG6 and PVRF6 depending on engine used. A Cheshire operator, Hollinshead, favoured Metalcraft bodywork on his PVRF6 coach, while Plaxton supplied coach-

work for a PVRG6 with Moffats of Stenhousemuir. PVR models had the radiator positioned behind the rear wheels on the off-side and clients could choose either a four or five speed constant mesh gearbox. Coachbuilders reacted favourably to the rear mounted engine, which allowed greater scope in body design. Overseas purchasers of Foden single deckers included organisations in Jamaica, Nigeria and South Africa.

FODEN/NORTHERN COUNTIES DOUBLE DECKER Foden's last bus of the 1950s was a PVD6 for Warrington. Many observers thought this signified the demise of passenger vehicle production, but in 1976 Foden stated their intention of building a new type of double decker in co-operation with the famous Northern Counties firm of Lancashire. Derby City Transport, PMT, West Yorkshire and Greater Manchester P.T.E. had examples, the latter authority acquiring the prototype in June 1976. However, it was surprising that only eight Foden/Northern Counties double deckers were manufactured, since ease of maintenance and exceptionally strong chassis seemed worthwhile qualities in a double deck bus. The chassis has a long perimeter frame which goes over the wheelarches so reinforcing the overall strength of the vehicle. Power comes from a Gardner 6LXB unit with Allison MT 640 automatic transmission together with an air cooled retarder.

A Foden-NC double decker (1979) with PMT, passing through the Potteries.

FORD

Perhaps more famous for its cars and trucks, Ford have made several ventures into the passenger vehicle market, including one vehicle based on the Model T chassis, and the AF model. However, the company ceased PSV production during the early 1930s, not coming on the scene again until the 1960s with the Thames Trader.

THAMES TRADER The Thames Trader employed proven Ford engines already popular in the company's trucks and passenger vehicles. The dimensions of the PSV chassis are a 17 ft. 6 in. long wheelbase and a 7 ft. 6 in. wide bodywork accommodating up to four people, the coachwork being supplied by companies such as Plaxton, Harrington and Duple. A longer model appeared in 1964 with an 18 ft. 2 in. wheelbase,

the engine being placed forward of the front wheels. The U.S. Air Force in the U.K. was one employer of the Thames Traders for passenger purposes.

MINIBUSES Ford Transits feature strongly in the small passenger vehicle range. Developed by a multi-national team in the early 1960s, and coming on the scene in 1965, the popular nine seater 'Custom' bus of 1970 is powered by a 1.7 litre engine, while the LWB 175 chassis carried a small vehicle with sixteen seats, and was powered by a

A Ford R226 (1968) displaying Willowbrook bodywork, used for stage carriage work by Wolverhampton Corporation.

Ford 2.4 litre diesel. During the early 1970s London Transport were asked by the G.L.C. to run minibus services in certain areas and soon FS types came on the streets with Strachan conversion body for services with little traffic, powered by Ford 2.2 litre diesel engines. The design of the Transit lends itself to modification not only as a passenger carrying vehicle but also as a tourer or a customised van, so popular in Europe today.

FORD R SERIES In the late 1960s Ford launched the R series 37 ft. chassis with fifty-three seat body provided by Duple. By the early 1970s Ford R series were seen with private coach operators and also with Alexander Northern, a member of the Scottish Bus Group whose fifty-three seater vehicles had bodywork by Alexander of Falkirk.

Wolverhampton Corporation Transport favoured the Ford R226 for bus work in the late 1960s. Plaxton were also responsible for supplying bodywork to a number of R series coaches such as the R114 range used by Coventry Corporation in the early 1970s. More recently, the R series may be seen with Midland Red, Smiths Happiway–Spencers, and Shearings Ribblesdale, with bodywork coming from Willowbrook and other famous coachbuilders. Recent R series feature the Ford 6 litre Turbo 11 diesel whose exhaust gases drive the turbo charger at about 90,000 rpm, so forcing air into engine cylinders at up to twice atmospheric pressure.

Willowbrook body on a Ford 192, acquired in 1970 by Garelochhead Coach Services, Scotland.

GUY

In 1914 Sydney Guy resigned as works manager of the Sunbeam Motor Company of Wolverhampton in order to start his own company, Guy Motors Ltd., which began to manufacture a variety of products ranging from aero engines to cars equipped with the new Guy V-8 engine. Following the First World War a charabanc was produced with accommodation for thirty people, and in 1923 Guy Motors introduced a one man operated bus, followed by vehicles such as Britain's first six wheeler double decker in 1926, a long distance sleeper coach in 1928 and the famous Guy Arab chassis for single and double decker buses in 1933. Guy Motors were one of only a few companies allowed to make chassis during the Second World War. The Arab I, powered by a Gardner 5LW oil engine, was introduced in 1942 and in the following year the

Arab II appeared, having a larger bonnet than the Mark 1 which facilitated the optional use of a Gardner 6LW engine. Arab II production ended in 1948. The Arab II served with groups including Midland Red, Southdown, East Yorkshire, Swindon, Grimsby and Devon General, this last company displaying vehicles with Roe H56R bodywork. In 1945 improved models of the Wolf and Vixen were introduced as buses and trucks, and Guy set about the production of a variety of single and double decker buses.

The firm acquired the Sunbeam Trolleybus Company Ltd. in 1947, but in 1961 Jaguar Cars Ltd. bought Guy Motors (Europe). The Jaguar group was absorbed by the British Motor Cor-

A Guy Arab II/Northern Counties, built in 1948 for use by Southdown.

This Park Royal bodied Guy Arab III was acquired by the Northern General Transport Company in 1952.

poration in 1967, later known as British Motor Holdings, which, in turn, merged with the Leyland Motor Group to become the British Leyland Motor Corporation. Recent years have seen the company operating under the name British Leyland Truck and Bus Division, Guy Motors. It is essential to note that during Guy's history a number of 'firsts' can be attributed to the group — the first charabanc, the first emergency exit door on buses before it was compulsory, and Britain's first six wheel double decker and trolleybus.

Arab Buses

ARAB III When peace came, the restrictions on the use of aluminium alloys were lifted allowing Guy to produce their Arab III double deck chassis. This improved version in the Arab series incorporated features such as a lighter chassis, and a lower mounted, polished aluminium radiator carrying an Indian Chief's head on the radiator filler cap. Coming with a variety of chassis types, Arab III buses were common sights with many operators in Britain, including Darlington, Durham, and Northern General. Blackburn had Northern Coachworks bodies, Tynemouth and District had Pickering fifty-six seat bodies, Mid-

A Guy Arab III single decker, new to Central S.M.T. in 1950, now restored to Western S.M.T. livery.

land Red employed Guy built fifty-six seat bodies, and Edinburgh favoured Metropolitan–Cammell H56R bodywork.

Engines for the Mark III range were Gardner 5LW or 6LW, and the Meadows 10.35 litre six cylinder oil engine which was more powerful than the Gardner 6LW — 115 bhp at 1,800 rpm. With a 16 ft. 3 in. wheelbase the Arab III had a length of 26 ft. and widths of 8 ft. or 7 ft. 6 in. A 27 ft. long bus with a 16 ft. 2 in. wheelbase followed in 1950. In 1948 an optional four speed pre-selector gearbox was introduced, and Red and

White had some five speed Meadows constant mesh gearboxes in their Arab III fleet. Some older Arabs were updated, Cheltenham District, for instance, in 1950 reconditioning a Mark II, equipping it with a Mark III front end and radiator.

A number of authorities preferred the Arab III single deck vehicles which came on the market in 1946. They were used by groups such as Lancashire United with Northern Counties and Roe C35F bodywork, Aberdare with Northern Counties body, Central SMT, and Burton whose Guy Arab III single deck buses were equipped with Guy B35R coachwork.

ARAB IV In 1950 Guy presented the Arab IV. Lancashire United were the first to purchase this model complete with Weymann H57R bodies, while other operators included, Chester, Southdown, and Birmingham, who bought over three hundred models; Cardiff, and Sunderland with Crossley bodies; Exeter with Massey H58R and H57R bodywork, and East Kent. Some versions were sent abroad, Kenya Omnibus Services receiving Arab IVs in the 1950s and South Africa taking delivery of Arab IV single deck buses, none of which was sold to U.K. authorities.

At first designed to meet the needs of Birmingham City Transport, the Arab IV came with a 27 ft. long body and 16 ft. 4 in. wheelbase, available in 7 ft. 6 in. or 8 ft. wide dimensions. During 1956 a 30 ft. long chassis with an 18 ft. 6 in. wheelbase was introduced when the law allowed it. Arab IVs received power from a variety of engines, the Gardner 5LW and 6LW and Meadows 10.35 litre 6DC630. Brakes were either of the vacuum aided triple servo variety or air brakes as, for example, with the 30 ft. long chassis. There was some overlap in production of Marks III and IV Arabs until 1953, in which year an exposed radiator was available for Mark IV buses for those customers who favoured this version. Production of the Arab IV was discontinued in 1960, although some buses were built in 1962 but by then the Wulfrunian and Arab Mark V were challenging the popularity of their predecessor.

ARAB V Guy realised the potential and demand for easy entrance loading on double deck buses and consequently brought out the Arab Mark V,

modifying the chassis, and reducing the number of entrance steps to only two. The Mark V came as a 30 ft. vehicle whose frame height was dropped by $2\frac{1}{2}$ in. to 1 ft. $9\frac{1}{2}$ in, thus making entry easier, especially on front entrance loaders. Power for Mark V Arabs came from Gardner LW/LX engines. Examples were seen in U.K. and overseas markets, some going to China, others to Lancashire United Transport with Northern Counties bodies, Cardiff, and Wolverhampton who had a number of bodybuilders including Strachans. The last Guy Arab buses to come into service in England were the three with Northern Counties bodies and 6LW engines and accommo-

This Guy Arab V/Northern Counties was received in 1964 by Lancashire United (left).

Guy Wolf with Barnaby B20F body built in 1948 for Llandudno U.D.C. (below).

dating seventy-three seated passengers purchased by Chester in 1969.

ARAB UF Guy valued the single deck bus market and in 1950 launched the Arab UF, an underfloor engined vehicle with a wheelbase of 16 ft. 4 in., either a Gardner 5HLW or 6HLW engine, and air brakes or triple servo vacuum brakes. A number of operators acquired UF buses during the production period of 1950–59, including Red and White whose fourteen vehicles had Duple Roadmaster bodies (DS852 KW040), Western and Central SMT with Alexander bodywork, Southampton with Park Royal B36D bodies and Huddersfield, plus a member of foreign authorities including Durban (Duple bodies) and Dar es Salaam with Guy bodywork.

Guy GS (NLLVP) with Eastern Coach Works body, delivered to London Transport in 1954.

WOLF, VIXEN AND SEAL The Guy Wolf first appeared in the 1930s, but production of the chassis was suspended during the Second World War. Coming with four cylinder engines, the Wolf and Vixen models had 13 ft. and 14 ft. 9 in. wheelbase measurements respectively, the Wolf carrying a Perkins P4 engine from 1952 onwards or a Guy petrol engine.

Companies employing Wolf buses included Llandudno Urban District Council, whose bodywork came from firms such as Barnaby, Metalcraft, and Roberts.

During 1959 Guy manufactured a small, underfloor engined chassis, the Seal, for the export market, in evidence, for instance, in Portugal. With a six cylinder Perkins oil engine, the Seal had either twenty-four seat or thirty to thirty-two seats and a 13 ft. wheelbase. It was based on the Vixen in that it had that models's spiral bevel rear axle.

GS BUSES In 1954 London Transport took delivery of eighty-four 'Special' Guy chassis designated NLLVP, this GS class being designed two years earlier, based on the Vixen with its rear axle, gearbox and chassis, but having a 15 ft. wheelbase. It was powered by a Perkins P6, 4.73 litre engine. Eastern Coachworks supplied their B26F body for the GS single deck bus which was popular on London routes such as the 329 to Knebworth, 309 to Garston, and 481 to Epsom. It is interesting to note that Ford bonnet and wings were employed on GS vehicles to give an up to date look.

OTTER Guy brought a new bus, the Otter, to the attention of operators in 1950, as a forward control single deck chassis with a number of engine choices available, including a Gardner 4LK oil or Guy's 3.8 litre petrol model. Chassis types were referred to as LLO (with petrol engines), LLOD (Gardner 4LK engines), and LLODP (Perkins engines). A four speed gearbox was standard, but the bevel rear axle had as an alternative the Eaton two speed model. Servo assisted hydraulic brakes were used. Bearing some exterior similarity to the Guy GS bus, the Otter had bodywork from companies such as Alexander and Mulliner. Overseas buyers for the Otter included East Africa, Belgium, South Africa and Holland, while on the domestic scene Douglas Corporation received models with Mulliner B26F bodies and distinctive destination indicators on the roof and on the side of the bus. Llandudno Corporation took delivery of two Otters with Roe twenty-six seat bodies powered by Gardner 4LK engines, and today Aberconwy U.D.C. still employ them for tourist trips.

LUF/WARRIOR LUF While UF Guy buses were in production, the company introduced the LUF in 1953 whose wheelbase was 16 ft. 4 in., power coming from a horizontally mounted Gardner 5HLW or 6HLW oil engine. Examples of LUF buses were found in the Neath and Cardiff Coach Firm with Park Royal bodywork, and in Aberdare, where vehicles had the Longwell Green body design.

During 1956 production of the Warrior LUF commenced with specifications similar to those of the Warrior truck chassis, but lighter than that employed in the LUF. It had a Meadows four cylinder, 5.43 litre oil engine and five speed gearbox. An A.E.C. 7.69 litre engine was later offered as an option. Bodywork was supplied for the Warrior by a number of firms including Mulliner, Burlingham and Willowbrook. Examples of Warrior buses could be observed with companies such as Castle Coaches and Dodds Coaches.

WULFRUNIAN At the 1959 Commercial Motor Show the public viewed the Guy Wulfrunian double deck chassis complete with front mounted engine alongside the driver and entrance facilities forward of the front axle — two years or so previously Guy had discussed plans for a low height double bus, particularly as other companies were already making moves in this direction, with Dennis 'Loline', Bristol 'Lodekka' and A.E.C. 'Bridgemaster' serving as examples. In an attempt to improve passenger comfort Guy installed Cave-Browne-Cave heating, using engine heated water pumped up to two radiators positioned on either side of the bus at the front of the top deck. Air coming through the front panel louvres was heated and ducted into the bus, while shutters diverted heat outside via side louvres in hot weather. The designers aimed to provide a 20 degrees Fahrenheit temperature in the bus.

Engines offered were Gardner 6LW and 6LX models or a Leyland 0.600 engine. With the 6LX engine, automatic gearbox and full fuel tank a Wulfrunian chassis weighed only five tons, and weighed 8 tons $11\frac{1}{2}$ cwts. with a Roe seventy-two seat body installed. Air suspension was fitted to all wheels together with hydraulically operated disc brakes. The first chassis appeared in 1959, equipped with Roe body painted in red and cream for use with West Riding Automobile Company (OHL 683). With an overall height of 13 ft. $4\frac{7}{8}$ in., the step height was only $14\frac{1}{2}$ in. from the ground allowing easy access. Two other chassis were constructed after this first model, receiving Roe bodywork in 1960, one accommodating seventy-two passengers, the other seventy-eight.

Initially with a wheelbase of 15 ft. 4 in., 17 ft. and 18 ft. versions were introduced in 1959 and 1960 respectively. Accrington Corporation were the sole purchaser of 28 ft. long rear entrance Wulfrunians, built on a 16 ft. wheelbase chassis with East Lancashire sixty-six seat body.

West Riding became the major purchaser of Guy Wulfrunians although it must be noted that other operators had examples. Chassis number 74716 with East Lancashire body went to Wolverhampton in 1961, and West Wales also received an East Lancashire version in the same year while Accrington acquired their Wulfrunians towards the end of that year. Later on, other companies bought Wulfrunians from original owners and ex-West Riding buses could be seen with operators at Hemel Hempstead in 1968, Dunfermline in 1974 and High Wycombe in 1970.

A Guy Otter with Mulliner B26F bodywork, built in 1957, seen here re-registered after service with Douglas Corporation.

Guy thought they had a best seller in the Wulfrunian and indeed its design and passenger comfort facilities were impressive, while its competitive price should have encouraged sales: in 1960 the Gardner 6LX engine model was £3,500, while the Leyland Atlantean 9.8 engine bus was £3,680. However, only 165 Wulfrunians were ordered with 137 built, production coming to an end in 1965, and questions were asked concerning the lack of general support for what appeared to be a modern and reliable vehicle. Some factors to be considered included the expense of renewing brake pads more frequently than on other buses, problems with front suspension units and, perhaps most important, Guy's acquisition by Jaguar Cars in 1961, which underlined the financial problems facing Guy.

TRAMBUS The Warrior Trambus chassis was based on the straight framed goods chassis and when the Warrior gave way to the Big J range a Trambus version made its appearance. Although mainly employed as a single deck vehicle, South Africa received double deck versions in the early 1970s. In 1975 the Guy Plant ceased building vehicles, concentrating on group components and the Trambus, renamed Victory I, was exhibited at the 1976 Commercial Motor Show with a Leyland engine. Examples of the Trambus/Victory can be seen overseas in areas such as Cape Town, who have double deck buses, and Zambia.

TROLLEY BUSES In 1926 Guy brought out the four wheel BT, which was in production until the early 1950s, and introduced the three axle BTX in 1927. In the years following 1945 a number of trolleybuses were manufactured by Guy, including seventy BTX vehicles, between 1947 and 1950, all for Belfast Corporation with Harkness bodies and G.E.C. electrical gear. The BT proved popular in such places as Wolverhampton, who ordered fifty with Park Royal bodies from 1949 onwards. In 1948 Guy acquired the Sunbeam Trolleybus Co. Ltd. (page 133).

Two Guy Otter chassis buses with Roe twenty-six seat bodies were acquired by Llandudno Corp. in 1954 (right).

Guy Wulfrunian with Roe bodywork seen in West Riding livery, 1963 (below).

JENSEN

November 1948 witnessed the inception of Jensen's JNSN forty seat coach chassis whose wheelbase was 16 ft. 2 in. in length. A Perkins PS engine was positioned vertically at the front. Bodywork was provided by companies such as Associated Coachbuilders. Jensen, however, tended to concentrate on trucks rather than passenger vehicles, consequently occupying only a small portion of the bus/coach market.

KARRIER

Pre 1939 models of Karrier passenger vehicles included the WL6 in service with Ashton-under-Lyne Corporation during the 1930s. Following the war a fourteen seat passenger chassis made its appearance, at first having a four cylinder Commer engine which was replaced in 1960 by the Standard $2\frac{1}{4}$ cylinder model. Some foreign operators favoured Karrier vehicles, such as a Swiss group whose vehicles had Rootes TS3 diesel engines (Rootes having bought Karrier in the 1930s), while a 'Gamecock' chassis, also powered by Rootes engines, proved popular in South Africa.

TROLLEYBUSES The three axle E6 appeared in 1928, the E4 in 1930, and the Karrier W in 1942. The end of the war saw an F4 model manufactured with both Karrier and Sunbeam nameplates. With either 16 ft. 3 in. or 17 ft. 6 in. wheelbases, and capable of carrying either double or single deck bodywork, it served in such places as Walsall, Derby, Ipswich and Wolverhampton. The F4 remained in production until 1952. During its period of manufacturing trolleybuses, Karrier worked in conjunction with a variety of bodybuilders including Roe, East Lancashire and Park Royal. In fact, Huddersfield was an authority having all three body types on its Karrier Trolleybuses, such as the E6 and MS2 series.

LEYLAND

The first steam wagon to be constructed and operated in Leyland was in use in 1884 but the story of Leyland Motors Ltd. commenced in 1896 when the Locomotives on Highways Act permitted vehicles of three tons solo weight and four tons with a trailer on the roads. After the First World War domestic and foreign orders for buses flooded in. At the 1925 Olympic Commercial Vehicle Show a collection of passenger vehicles comprising the forward control single deck Lion bus, the Leviathan double decker and the Lionness coach, attracted tremendous interest.

Subsequent pre 1939 buses included the Leyland Cub KP3 and KP03, built at Leyland's Kingston on Thames factory between 1931 and 1936, and the Lion L73 (1931) with a 17 ft. 6 in. wheelbase and Leyland four cylinder petrol engine, examples serving with Rawtenstall Corporation Transport. The Titan TD2 of 1931 was a double decker powered by a Leyland 7.6 litre petrol engine, Jersey, Southdown and Portsmouth possessing examples, while the Cub KP2, a 14 ft. wheelbase single decker, saw work with

companies such as Crosville. The Lion LT5 again had a Leyland engine and the Olympic Show of 1933 gave the public the opportunity to view Leyland's oil engines. The Titan TD3 also came on the scene in 1933 featuring the re-designed Leyland radiator of a deeper model with parallel sides. Other examples of buses in the 1930s included the Leyland Beaver TSC9, the Tiger TS6 (1933), Cub KPZ2 of 1935 and the Lion LT7 of the same year, the double deck Titan TD4, the TEPI or 'Gnu' with twin steering axles and 8.6 diesel engine, and two years later the 'Panda'. In the years leading up to the Second World War Leyland manufactured several models including the Tiger TS7T, the Lion LT8, Tiger TS8, and the Titan TD7, a double decker launched in 1939 which served with operators such as Birmingham, Lincoln and West Hartlepool, this last authority favouring Roe H48C bodywork. Rather interest-

Leyland PS1/Alexander thirty-four seat body, purchased by Central S.M.T. in 1949, sold in 1964, engine type E181 no. 2304.

ingly a 1935 Leyland Tiger T57 carrying 1948 Weymann coachwork was put on the run by Yorkshire Traction in 1981 for rallying and excursions.

Leyland's interesting history has many instances of expansion and the acquisition of other firms. For example, after the Second World War, Leyland Motors took over West Yorkshire Foundries in Leeds, and the company of British United Traction Ltd. was jointly owned by A.E.C. and Leyland, while the long established Scottish vehicle group Albion Motors was acquired in 1951. During 1955 the shareholders of Scammell Lorries Ltd., Watford, agreed to terms for the acquisition of the company's entire share issue capital by Leyland Motors. In 1962 Leyland integrated with one of their biggest U.K. rivals — Associated Commerical Vehicles Ltd., producers of A.E.C. trucks and buses, including Park Royal vehicles, the Maudslay Motor Company Ltd., and Transport Equipment (Thornycroft) Ltd.

In recent years Leyland Truck and Bus have won many orders, such as a £13.1 million order from Iran in 1975 and four hundred National buses delivered to Venezuela. Trends in bus design include the Titan and Olympian plus the bus chassis, B43, the Leyland Tiger of the 1980s.

Single deckers

PS1 The PS1 or Tiger appeared in 1946. It had an overall length of 27 ft. 6 in. on a 17 ft. 6 in. wheelbase and a high straight frame extension behind the rear axle, the PS1/1 featuring a dropped extension adaptable as a luggage locker on coaches or as a rear entrance on passenger vehicles. Receiving power from Leyland 7.4 litre six cylinder oil engines, PS1 vehicles came with four speed constant mesh gearboxes, fully floating rear axles and vacuum servo brakes. The PS1/1 and PS1/4 had 210 in. wheelbases, while the PS1/13 225 in. version was capable of carrying a body

A Crosville Leyland Tiger PS1/1 equipped with Weymann DP35F bodywork, built in 1950.

with a length of 360 in.. Some instances of operators and body types are as follows:

Operator	Chassis	Body Type
N. Ireland Road Transport Board	PS1	N. I. Road Transport Board B34R
Central S.M.T.	PS1	Alexander 34 seat
Alexander P.A.	PS1	Alexander C35F
Yorkshire Woollen District Transport	PS1	Duple A
Leeds City Transport	PS1	Roe B36R
Southdown	PS1/1	Eastern Coachworks B32R
Southdown	PS1/1	Park Royal C32R
Crosville	PS1/1	Weymann DP35F

COMET (CPP1 AND CPO1) In December 1947 Leyland Motors announced a new range of modern Comet trucks and buses originally designated for overseas markets but proving popular with domestic authorities and transport groups. The Comet series heralded Leyland's new frontal styling and design, all models having semi-forward controls allowing for the ideal compromise on medium weight trucks and buses between length, accessibility to the engine, and weight distribution. The designation 'Comet' came from the tank of the same name designed and built by Leyland Motors during the Second World War. The normal control chassis could accommodate up to thirty-three passengers in 7 ft. 6 in. and 8 ft. wide versions with either a 15 ft. 10 in. or 17 ft. 6 in. wheelbase. Leyland engines were again featured in the Comet bus, the CPO1 using the 0.300 model while a P.300 version was employed in CPP1 vehicles, both coming with vacuum hydraulic brakes and five speed gearboxes. The range remained in production until 1951.

The following year saw Leyland change the domestic Comet model, upgrading it to a forward control vehicle with full width cab and no separate bulkhead, having the more substantial O.350 90 bhp engine and optional wheelbases — 16 ft. 11 in. for ECPO2/1 versions and 14 ft. 8 in. for the ECPO2/2 variety, accommodating 27.6 ft. and 25 ft. long bodywork respectively. A further title was that of ECPO2/1T when equipped with a two speed rear axle, and buyers had a choice of a single of Eaton two speed axle.

TIGER OPS2 The year 1948 was important for Leyland in that the industrial units division was set up, and about this time British Road Services was formed, to whom Leyland Motors Ltd. sold many heavy and medium vehicles. On the passenger front, Leyland brought out a forward control single deck chassis in the form of the Tiger OPS2 powered by a Leyland O.600 series, 9.8 litre engine with four speed synchromesh gearbox, and fitted with triple servo vacuum brakes. Both coach and bus versions had a 17 ft. 6 in. wheelbase and were 8 ft. wide.

TIGER PS2 Leyland were expert at accommodating customer specifications and, when they

A Leyland PS2/5 new to Ribble Motor Services in 1950 as a thirty-five seater Burlingham bodied bus, withdrawn from service in 1964, and converted to a PSV recovery unit.

Leyland Tiger PS2/3 exhibiting Windover C32F body, built in 1950.

introduced the PS2 in 1948, soon saw the potential of offering the basic chassis with alternative options as demanded by clients, a factor seen in many Leyland passenger products. Several body builders demonstrated their interest in the Tiger PS2, with East Lancashire Coachworks, for instance, supplying many PS2/14s to Burnley, Nelson and Colne Transport Authority in 1953–54, while Burlingham, Roe, Metropolitan-Cammell, A.C.B. and Windover were further instances of body builders working with the Tiger PS2.

Private operators expressed a keen interest in the PS2 and, consequently, Leyland called their 7 ft. 6 in. wide chassis PS2/1 if employed for bus duties and PS2/3 for coach work. The PS2 chassis was similar to that of the PS1 model but accommodated a larger Leyland six cylinder 9.8 litre oil engine together with a four speed gearbox, and, though starting off with a 17 ft. 6 in. wheelbase, an 18 ft. 9 in. version was offered in 1950, allowing for a 30 ft. long overall length. Such variations in design brought about multifarious titles for particular marques, as indicated by the following examples taken from the PS2 range of vehicles:

Title	Chassis Width	Bus/Coach	Wheelbase
PS2/5	8 ft. 0 in.	Bus	17 ft. 6 in.
PS2/7	8 ft. 0 in.	Coach	17 ft. 6 in.
PS2/12	8 ft. 0 in.	Bus	18 ft. 9 in.
PS2/13	8 ft. 0 in.	Coach	18 ft. 9 in.
PS2/14	7 ft. 6 in.	Bus	18 ft. 9 in.
PS2/15	7 ft. 6 in.	Coach	18 ft. 9 in.

ROYAL TIGER PSU1 The Leyland Royal Tiger underfloor chassis appeared in 1950, starting a

trend towards similar chassis types, and, at the 1950 Commercial Motor Show, Dennis, Guy and Atkinson also displayed underfloor models. Partly to combat this competition and to accommodate the many demands from a variety of customers, Leyland made nine variations based on the PSU1 underfloor engined chassis, including the PSU1/15, an 8 ft. wide coach version, and the PSU1/16, a similar model having air brakes instead of vacuum brakes. The original chassis was 15 ft. 7 in. long, receiving power from a Leyland 9.8 litre six cylinder oil engine with a four speed synchromesh gearbox, and was available in 7 ft. 6 in. and 8 ft. widths; in April 1954 a bigger 11.1 litre 0.680 engine horizontal engine was offered as an option with a pneumo-cyclic gearbox, together with diaphragm operated air brakes.

In the first half year of production, the Royal Tiger found buyers in many markets around the world. Two hundred operators placed orders, including Ripponden and District whose 1951 PSU1/15, with bodywork by Associated Coach-builders of Sunderland, later went to Hebble, while some Ribble PSU1/13 and PSU1/15 vehicles had Leyland bodies. PSU1/13 models were also observed with Southdown who acquired a new bus in 1952 with a forty seat, rear entrance body, and a Duple Roadmaster bodied forty-one seat PSU1/15 supplied to Standerwick in 1951 went to the parent Ribble fleet in 1963.

OLYMPIC Royal Tiger and Olympic underfloor engined passenger models were displayed in 1950 and it could be argued that they contributed to the virtual demise of the U.K. market for vertical engined single deck buses. The Olympic followed on from the 1949 HR40 and had its 9.8 litre six cylinder Leyland engine positioned underfloor amidships. Its 15 ft. 7 in. wheelbase came in both 7 ft. 6 in. and 8 ft. widths, the integral constructed vehicle seating forty-four people. Ribble again proved a good customer.

The Olympic was produced in conjunction with Metropolitan-Cammell-Weymann and the domestic series of 15 ft. 7 in. wheelbase chassis was known as the HR40 while the 1950 15 ft. 7 in.

A North Western Leyland Royal Tiger PSU1/15 with Leyland body, 1952.

100

wheelbase for 30 ft. length bodies had the title
HR44. U.K. versions of the Olympic possessed
a doorway ahead of the front axle while overseas buses featured two doors, one in front of
each axle.

*A Weymann B44F bodied Leyland Tiger Cub
PSUC1/1.*

TIGER CUB PSUC1 To meet a demand for
buses of lighter weights than previous models a
new chassis type was introduced in the form of
A.E.C.'s Reliance of 1953. Leyland countered
with the Tiger Cub, offering a smaller engine than
those found with competitors, the 5.80 litre 0350.
In 1959 an alternative engine was presented,
Leyland's own six cylinder 6.17 litre model, while
1963 saw the introduction of a 6.54 litre six
cylinder oil engine. The Tiger Cub found favour

with numerous bus and coach operators including the following:

Operator	Chassis	Body Type
Bournemouth	PSUCl/2T	Burlingham
Ribble	PSUC1/1	Saunders-Roe
Ribble	PSUC1/2	Burlingham
North Western	PSUC1/1	Weymann
Ulster Transport Authority	PSUC1/5T	Saunders-Roe

The designations for chassis type depended on a number of factors such as the clutch used or whether it was a coach or bus version, including:

Chassis	Specifications
PSUC1/1	16 ft. 2 in. wheelbase; 8 ft. wide; bus version with extended chassis.
PSUC1/2	As above, except it was a coach model without the extension.
PSUC1/3	16 ft. 2 in. wheelbase; 8 ft. wide; 4 speed gearbox.
PSUC1/4 (1955)	16 ft. 2 in. wheelbase; 7 ft. 6 in. wide; 4 speed gearbox.
PSUC1/5	Same as PSUC1/4, except it had 2 speed rear axle instead of single speed.
OPSUC1/3 (1953)	Export version of the PSUC1/3; capable of carrying bus coachwork.
PSUC1/11 (1963)	Bus version with 6.54 litre oil engine; 4 or 5 speed gearbox; one or 2 speed rear axle.
PSUC1/12	Coach version of above.
PSUC1/13 (1963)	0.400 engine; 4 speed gearbox.

London Transport experimented with three lightweight vehicles, a Bristol LS5G, A.E.C. monocoach and a Leyland Tiger Cub (registration PTE 592) with Saunders Roe body. All three were based at Reigate Garage and were later returned to the manufacturers without further action being taken. The Tiger Cub was of the PSUC1/1 variety having air pressure cam brakes, a Leyland 0350 six cylinder 5.76 litre oil engine and room for forty-four seated passengers. The lack of interest shown by London was not reflected elsewhere and the Tiger Cub PSUC1 remained in production until 1969 after a run of seventeen years.

PANTHER In response to 1961 legislation allowing 36 ft. long buses to travel on U.K. roads, Bedford brought out the 36 ft. VAL; the Bristol VE was a further instance of a longer single deck bus. The A.E.C. Swift appeared as a low or high frame bus and Leyland's Panther buses also had this option, being 36 ft. in length and powered by a horizontally placed 9.8 litre engine, while the low frame Panther had a 6.5 litre 400 engine as employed in 33 ft. long buses. Northern General is an example of an authority employing Panthers, and in early 1981 some of these with Marshall Camair B48D bodies were withdrawn from service, as were a number in the Western National fleet which had Marshall B47D coachwork.

The Panther's engine and semi-automatic gearbox were placed under the floor at the rear of the chassis, thus keeping down the noise level and allowing for more equable weight distribution, consequently reducing wear on tyres and improving steering, braking and suspension. A prototype right hand drive Panther was used in service in Stockholm and in June 1965 Stockholm Tramways reinforced Leyland's name abroad by ordering two hundred Panthers and fifty Atlanteans.

LEOPARD At the Scottish Motor Show, towards the end 1959, Leyland demonstrated for the first time the medium weight Leopard chassis. The two versions offered both had the 0.600

A Leyland Panther PSUR1A/1 in service with Wigan (1969) equipped with Northern Counties bodywork (right).

Leyland Tiger Club, manufactured in 1958 for Viking Motors, with Willowbrook body (below).

horizontal engine, four speed synchromesh gearbox, optional two speed rear axle, and air brakes on all four wheels, and measured 8 ft. wide and 30 ft. overall long. The Ll type had a straight rear extension for bus work while the L2's dropped extension made it more suitable for coaches.

Sheffield and Western SMT of Kilmarnock were among the first purchasers of Leopard coaches, the latter employing twenty on the Glasgow to London trip which allowed Leyland to boast that on an average three thousand miles a week, the Leopard achieved seventeen miles to the gallon. Among the many users of Leopards, North Western had five Duple Commander III bodied coaches supplied in 1968, popular on the X97 route, while National Wessex also favoured a forty-nine seater with Duple Alpine continental

coachwork. Halifax employed a number of Leopards for stage carriage work on one man operated routes.

In October 1961 a 36 ft. long Leopard with 18 ft. 6 in. wheelbase was offered to clients with synchromesh gearbox and straight frame extension. Other versions included the PSU3/2, featuring fluid coupling, pneumo-cyclic gearbox and straight frame extension, the PSU3/3 with a dropped frame and synchromesh gearbox, and the PSU3/4 with dropped frame, together with the pneumo-cyclic gearbox.

Later Leopard designs were the PSU4/2 and PSU4/4 whose specifications included pneumo-cyclic gearboxes, and straight and dropped frame extensions respectively. The Ll and L2 marques were renamed PSU4/1 and PSU4/3. Today there

are numerous examples of private and municipal operators with Leyland Leopards, such as Smiths of Tysoe; Yorkshire Traction with Willowbrook bodies; National Potteries who have examples of the PSU3/4 with Duple bodywork; Nottingham City Transport who received a Duple Dominant E type with fifty-three seats in 1976, and Wallace Arnold whose coach WUG 128S has a Special Duple Dominant 1 forty-five seat body of 7 ft. $8\frac{1}{2}$ in. width.

The more recent PSU3F and PSU5D Leopards offer choices of length and transmission:

Model	Wheelbase	Length O/A	Transmission
3F.2R	18 ft. 6 in.	36 ft. 1 in.	Pneumo-cyclic
3F.4R	18 ft. 6 in.	36 ft. 1 in.	Pneumo-cyclic
3F.5R	18 ft. 6 in.	36 ft. 1 in.	Manual
5D.4R	20 ft. 0 in.	39 ft. 4 in.	Pneumo-cyclic
5D.5R	20 ft. 0 in.	39 ft. 4 in.	Manual

These boast heavy duty premium road chassis with in-built flexibility for varied jobs such as bus work, motorway express service or touring, and the heavy duty suspension is standard allowing GVW's of up to 16 tons, so that the chassis can be matched up to legal loading limits. The modern Leopard receives power from Leyland's 680 horizontal in-line diesel engine rated at 175 bhp at 2,200 rpm for coach work and 2,000 rpm for bus work. Bodybuilders favour the parallel sided flat top frame chassis which offers an unobstructed level surface and space at the rear of the chassis frame for coach-builders to provide a large rear luggage boot with space for side lockers. Drivers of the modern Leopard are assisted by a variety of standard features including power assisted steering which gives turning circles varying from seventy-one to seventy-eight feet, spring parking brakes operating on the driven axle, and semi-elliptic laminated leaf springs allowing for good roadholding and a smooth ride. Furthermore, eleven and twelve metre models are available with the ZF S6-80 manual gearbox — a direct drive unit of heavy duty construction mounted with the engine, whose ratios provide good restart capabilities and guarantee the maximum use of power.

A Leyland Leopard L2/Eastern Counties single decker acquired by Bolton Transport in 1962.

Leopard PSU5 coaches serve with firms such as Tatlock and Richards, while in mid 1981 Alexander (Fife) received Alexander bodied (B53F) Leopard PSU3.4R coaches.

NATIONAL 1 The Leyland National Company Ltd. had been formed in 1969 by British Leyland and the National Bus Company for the construction of an £8 million project at Workington, Cumbria, where a forty acre site was acquired containing one of the largest commercial vehicle production shops in Britain, employing the car type mechanised assembly methods for building buses. At a time when many authorities were considering replacing single deckers by double deck passenger vehicles, Leyland announced their

National single decker at the 1970 London Commercial Show. The bus was built at the Workington plant and attracted much initial attention since it was an integral bus suitable for automated production and giving structural safety.

The low floor National with rear mounted Leyland 8.2 litre 510 turbocharged engine was at first available in 10.3 m. or 11.3 m. lengths, the National Bus Company being an important buyer,

A PSU3F.4R Leyland Leopard with Duple body owned by National (Potteries), 1979 (right).

A Leyland Leopard with Willowbrook coachwork used for stage carriage work by Halifax, 1965 (below).

A Ribble Leyland National 2, 1980.

NATIONAL 2 Following on from the design award winning National of 1970, Leyland introduced the National 2 available in 10.6 or 11.6 m. lengths with power coming from the company's own 680H engine mounted at the rear, an 11.1 litre unit producing 170 bhp at 2,000 rpm. The standard transmission is the well-tested Leyland five speed, close ratio, semi-automatic, pneumo-cyclic gearbox, but fully automatic transmission is available as an option. Driver and passenger comfort feature high on Leyland's priority list and the raised floor in the cab affords the driver an unobstructed view of the entrance while easily visible controls and a system preventing movement if the exit door is open, all contribute to driver comfort and overall safety. Passengers board through a low step entrance and other features include large windows, glare free lighting and an automatic temperature control unit with up to eighty air changes an hour.

The Suburban Express is Leyland's National 2 with extra facilities for higher speed express work. This model exhibits high backed seats with head rests, full length luggage racks and fitted carpet as an option while the near side longitudinal seat can be replaced by a luggage container if required. It is interesting to note that National 2 vehicles can be adapted to a number of uses such as a mobile bank or library, a casualty unit, or a British Airways' passenger transit vehicle at London Airport with central exits on both sides, so encouraging quick disembarking. Numerous operators have National 2s including Trent, Ribble, Crosville and London, whose National 2s have now replaced A.E.C. Swifts and Merlins on some Red Arrow Services, the new Ash Grove garage being the first in London to operate the new National 2s on the Red Arrow routes 513 and 502.

THE NEW LEYLAND CUB The rising fuel costs of the 1980s have persuaded some operators to employ small PSV chassis of the twenty-three to thirty-three seat group and the modern Leyland Cub is admirably suited for this area of bus or coach work with wheelbase options as shown.

The Cub has many advantages over competitors in this range of chassis. The extended frame permits a front entrance, while a power steering option and wide front springs contribute to a vehicle whose frame allows coachbuilders to have

ordering five hundred buses at the Earls Court Show, where Australia, Fiji, Yugoslavia and Pakistan also placed orders. This sensible design was based on ergonomic studies to make access easier, and the air suspension contributed to a smooth and pleasant ride while wide windows, fluorescent lights and low noise levels, together with excellent heating and ventilation, all made for a best selling single decker.

Among the many fleet operators purchasing the National bus, London Transport introduced it in 1973 as a one man operated bus with a capacity for thirty-six seated and twenty-seven standing passengers plus separate front entrance and centre exit. Eventually, London had over four hundred Leyland Nationals in service. Other examples of companies with Leyland National included London Country, Crosville, Northampton Transport, and Maidstone and District (who in 1981 exchanged some with Southdown for Daimler Fleetlines). The many foreign buyers included Venezuela, where four hundred Nationals were used in the Caracas district, a sale worth £11 million in 1975 which was in fact equal to a tenth of Britain's annual bill for oil from Venezuela.

A Leyland Tiger of the 1980s, a prototype with Eastern Scottish with Duple Dominant III coachwork; the Leyland Badge was placed on this vehicle at a later date.

an exit of at least 21 in. wide and a bodied rear overhang up to 60 per cent of the wheelbase.

Model	Wheelbase	Turning Circle	G.V. Weight
CU 335	11 ft. 0 in.	48 ft. 0 in.	6.5 ton
CU 385	12 ft. 7½ in.	52 ft. 0 in.	8.5 ton
CU 435	14 ft. 3¼ in.	55 ft. 0 in.	8.5 ton

B43, LEYLAND TIGER The name Tiger reflects a long pedigree for the B43 premium coach chassis revealed to the public in 1981, going back to the Tiger TS1 of 1929 and moving through the PS series, Royal Tiger, Tiger Cub and Royal Tiger Worldmaster makes. A full colour tiger's head and the traditional Leyland scroll, in a more modern, somewhat more flattened form than earlier, appear on the badges, whilst Leopard style wheel trims are employed at the front with the updated Leyland scroll.

Evolving out of the Leopard and Reliance designs, the Tiger of the 1980s employs a straight flat topped robust chassis, with the frame finishing behind the rear suspension mounting to allow body design freedom at the rear end, and chassis are available for 12 m. or 11.3 m. overall length bodies. Power comes from Leyland's TL11H engine — an 11.1 litre six cylinder direct injection, in-line, turbocharged diesel unit mounted amidships beneath the floor. The standard full air suspension and anti-roll bars at the front provide smooth rides, while a huge front mounted radiator with automatic hydraulic fan keeps the engine cool from minus 20 to plus 36 degrees Centigrade. Driver and passenger comfort is of the highest standard, featuring refinements such as an 18 in. diameter steering wheel, side control box, and easily visible controls.

Double Deckers

TITAN PD1 Leyland's first double deck bus chassis after the war was known as the Titan, a PD1 chassis with few similarities to the pre-war models which bore the name Titan (such as the TD4), having a 16 ft. 3 in. wheelbase and width of 7 ft. 6 in.; an 8 ft. wide model, referred to as the PD1/3, appeared in 1946. Giving a fuel consumption of 14 mpg at 39 mph, the PD1 proved popular with a variety of operators, coming to them equipped with triple servo brakes and fully floating rear axle, the PD1A having rubber instead of metal bushes on the road spring shackle pins. Rather surprisingly under 2,000 PD1s were made, some pundits saying its 7.4 litre engine was not powerful enough. Examples of authorities with PD1 Titans included Lytham St. Annes, Ribble, Manchester, Eastbourne, Leicester, Hants and Dorset, and London who acquired some in 1946 as a stop gap until the RT vehicles arrived the following year, PD1s being based at garages such as Croydon, Victoria and Hanwell. Bodywork for PD1s came not only from outside concerns such as Eastern Coachworks, but also from Leyland itself.

TITAN PD2 Some would argue that the PD2 was one of the most popular British bus designs, with thirty eight variations built between 1947 and 1968 when production ceased. The PD2/1 was 7 ft. 6 in. wide while the PD2/3 measured 8 ft. in width, each marque having an overall length of 26 ft. and featuring vacuum servo brakes and four speed synchromesh gearbox, while the PD2/5 had facilities to accommodate full front entrance bodywork and air brakes. Leyland's 0.600 type six cylinder oil engine (9.8 litre) was employed.

When domestic buses were allowed to be 27 ft. in length Leyland increased the PD2 wheelbase to 16 ft. 5 in. and made the 7 ft. 6 in. wide PD2/10 and PD2/11 chassis with vacuum and air brakes respectively, and the 8 ft. wide models PD2/12 (vacuum brakes) and PD2/13 (air brakes). 1953 saw the introduction of the PD2/20 and PD2/21 versions featuring concealed radiators, the former having vacuum servo brakes, and the latter having air brakes. In the following year Leyland renamed

A Leyland Titan TD4, built in 1937 but later supplied with a new body in 1951.

Eastern Coach Works bodied Leyland PD1 (above).

A Leyland PD2/1 with 1948 Leyland bodywork, in service with Lytham St. Annes (below).

the PD2/10 and 11, the PD2/22 and 23 respectively, and two new models were introduced, the PD2/24 and 25, respectively 8 ft. and 7 ft. 6 in. wide, equipped with Leyland's pneumo-cyclic direct air shift semi-automatic four speed epicyclic gearbox.

During the mid 1950s domestic PD2s were provided with 8 in. instead of the 9 in. worm centres for the rear axle and PD2/20, 21, 22, and 23 were re-titled PD2/30, 27, 31 and 38 respectively. The PD2/37 of 1956 had an exposed radiator and air brakes while the PD2/40 and 41 of the same year carried concealed radiators together with vacuum servo brakes and synchromesh gearboxes. A further variation of the mid-1950s came in the form of the PD2/34 which had an exposed radiator, pneumo-cyclic gearbox and air brakes. PD2A/24 buses featured a 197 in. wheelbase, 324 in. body length and fibreglass fronts and were made in the years 1960-67. All 7 ft. 6 in. models were stopped from 1962 but 8 ft. versions continued in production until 1968

with the suffixes 24, 27, 30, 34, 37 and 40.

The large number of models assured work for many coachbuilders. Some examples are given below:

Body Type	Chassis	Operator
Alexander	PD2/20	Liverpool Corporation
Burlingham	PD2/5	Blackpool
	PD2/12	Ribble
	PD2/34	Manchester Corporation
East Lancashire	PD2/3	Ribble
	PD2/20	Rawtenstall Corporation
	PD2/40	Haslingden
Leyland	PD2/1	Lytham St. Annes
	PD2/12	Trent Motor Traction
Massey Bros	PD2/37	Baxters, Lanarkshire
Metropolitan-Cammell	PD2/3	Manchester
	PD2/12	Astill and Jordan
	PD2/40	Portsmouth; Plymouth
Northern Counties	PD2/12	Southdown
	PD2/20	Alexander (Northern)
Roe	PD2/3	Trent Motor Traction
	PD2/12	Trent Motor Traction
	PD2/30	Sheffield
Weymann	PD2/12	N. Western R.C.C.
	PD2/21	N. Western R.C.C.
	PD2/37	Brighton
	PD2/40	Liverpool Corporation

Naturally there are not many PD's in service these days and Barrow Transport ceased double deck operations in 1980, withdrawing 1961 Leyland PD2A/27s with Massey H37/27F bodies, and in 1981 Halton withdrew its PD2/40 (registration number HTF 645B) with East Lancashire body (H37/28R).

A Leyland PD2/12, new to Rawtenstall Corporation in 1953 and not withdrawn from service until 1974 (top).

A Leyland PD2/20 with Alexander bodywork, acquired by Liverpool Corporation in 1954 (bottom).

This Bradford City Transport Karrier trolleybus features a W chassis of 1945 plus East Lancashire H66FD bodywork of 1965 (above).

Belonging to the McLennon group, this 1951 Leyland single decker is from the PS1 series (below).

A Leyland National 2 owned by Trent Motor Traction Company (above).

A Duple Dominant 11 metre body is carried on this Leyland Leopard PSU3B/4R (below).

A Leyland Titan PD2/40 with East Lancashire coachwork, built in 1964 (above).

A Stockport Corporation PD3/14, built in 1969, carrying East Lancashire bodywork (below).

This Leyland PD3 (1958) displays Alexander bodywork. It is in service with Western S.M.T.

A Roe bodied Atlantean PDR1/3 (1968) seen in service with Teesside.

Reading Borough Transport Leyland Titan, 1979.

*One of the China Motor Bus Company's two axle
M.C.W. buses.*

*Greater Manchester P.T.E. employs
Seddon/Pennine one man operated buses on the
Piccadilly Station to Victoria Station route.*

A 1980 D.A.F. 200 DKTL coach carrying Plaxton Supreme Mark IV coachwork.

One of Walsall's F4A Sunbeam trolleybuses with Willowbrook bodywork (above).

Van Hool coachwork is carried on this Volvo B10M vehicle (below).

OPD2 The undoubted popularity of the Titan PD2 encouraged Leyland to manufacture an export model in the form of a 17 ft. 6 in. wheelbase chassis known as the OPD2 powered by the company's 0.600 six cylinder 9.8 litre engine and featuring either air brakes or triple servo vacuum brakes.

PD3 The highly acclaimed PD2 series underlined the need for a longer model and with this in mind Leyland brought out the PD3, with a 30 ft. overall length on an 18 ft. 6 in. wheelbase, making its début in September 1956. Leyland's 9.8 litre six cylinder engine powered the PD3 series. In keeping with other Leylands, the PD3 had a number of variations, the PD3/1 having air brakes and synchromesh gearbox, and concealed radiator, while the PD3/2 featured a pneumo-cyclic gearbox. PD3A/1 buses, such as those with Leicester Corporation and Blackpool Corporation, were typified by a 222 in. wheelbase and a body length of 360 in. and were built between 1960 and 1966. The PD3/3 model carried a concealed radiator, vacuum brakes and four speed synchromesh gearbox, while the PD3/4 featured an exposed radiator; PD3/5 and PD3/6 buses had air brakes and vacuum brakes respectively. In 1962 the PD3/3 marque was discontinued. Five years later the series was renamed with the PD3/11 coming with concealed radiator and synchromesh gearbox, the PD3A/12 boasting a pneumo-cyclic gearbox, the exposed radiator models with synchromesh and pneumo-cyclic gearboxes being named PD3/14 and PD3A/15.

Bournemouth was an instance of an authority with PD3/1 Leyland buses, Leeds had PD3/5s on the run with Roe H70R bodywork and Ribble boasted PD3/4 vehicles with Burlingham bodywork, while the PD3A/2 bus was popular in places such as Bolton.

A Manchester Corporation Leyland PD2/34 double decker, built in 1958, with Burlingham bodywork (top).

Now with Merseyside P.T.E., this Leyland PD2/40 built in 1965, has a Weymann body (bottom).

One of Leicester Corporation's Leyland PD3A/1, Park Royal bodied buses, 1966 (above).

A Blackpool Corporation Leyland PD3A/1 vehicle equipped with Metropolitan–Cammell bodywork, 1966 (top right).

TITAN 7RT Built only for London Transport, who designated it 7RT, this bus was based on the PD2/1. London Transport received a prototype in May 1948, giving it a Park Royal body and numbering it RTL 501, the '501' allowing for five hundred Leyland RT production models which would be 8 ft. in width instead of 7 ft. 6 in. There would have been problems with two different

A Leyland PD3A/2 built in 1962 for Bolton Transport, passing to S.E.L.N.E.C. (Northern) in 1969 and eventually withdrawn in 1975. An unusual vehicle in that it features a full front instead of the normal half cab (bottom right).

A Yorkshire Traction Leyland Atlantean PDR1/2 equipped with a Northern Counties L75F body, and built in 1967.

widths of chassis in one bonnet code and before deliveries of the wider buses began they were provided with the letters RTW, the last letter signifying 'wide'. RTW vehicles had 8 ft. wide Leyland bodywork while the RTL versions came with Weymann, Park Royal and Metropolitan–Cammell–Weymann bodywork. RTL's had a laden weight of 11 tons 12 cwt., while the RTW's weighed 11 tons 16 cwt.

ATLANTEAN In 1952 Leyland tried out ideas for a rear engined double decker, with a maximum permitted width of 7 ft. 6 in. A Leyland 0.350 engine, turbocharged to increase power and provide performance equal to that of the 0.600 engine, was transversely mounted at the rear of the sub frame of a chassis which carried a platform type frame of steel and light alloy with deep stressed sidemembers. An automatic clutch and self change gearbox were fitted.

A variety of operators tested the pair of experimental rear engined double deckers and in 1953 a design committee looked at the possibility of constructing a bus whose features included low

A Leyland Atlantean 68.1R/Park Royal vehicle (1972) seen in Levenshulme on the 169 Greater Manchester P.T.E. route.

A Fleetline FE 30 AGR with Northern Counties body (1978) with Chester City Transport, seen in the city centre.

platform front entrance, rear engine and lower floor height. In 1956 the 0.600 diesel engine was put at the rear of the chassis across the frame with a centrifugal clutch or fluid flywheel, pneumocyclic gearbox and angle drive. Having an overall height of only 13 ft. $2\frac{3}{4}$ in., the bus had a 16 ft. $2\frac{7}{8}$ in. wheelbase with an overall length of 29 ft. 10 in. and could carry seventy-eight seated passengers. Two models of these prototype Atlanteans were thoroughly tested and throughout the development of the project Leyland engineers worked in liaison with Metropolitan-Cammell-Weymann whose designers offered many worthwhile suggestions. The result of this work was publicised at the 1958 Commercial Motor Show, the arena for the arrival of the Atlantean.

During 1958 Leyland launched the Atlantean

PDR1/1 bus with a standard front entrance and a 16 ft. 3 in. wheelbase as in the 1956 prototype. The Atlantean PDR1/1 found popularity with numerous operators such as P.M.T., and Birkenhead, whose fifteen Northern Countries models were one man operated, while across the Mersey Liverpool employed the model, as did Newcastle whose buses featured Alexander bodies, this same coachbuilder supplying bodywork for Glasgow Corporation Atlanteans. Northern Countries built bodies for authorities such as Yorkshire Traction while Roe bodied the Atlantean for Lancaster and Northern. Recent acquisition of Atlanteans have included examples with Alexander bodies H45/33F by Tyne and Wear in 1981, while about the same time, South Yorkshire received Marshall bodied Atlanteans. The Atlantean range was

A Leyland Olympian in service with Ribble (left).

as follows: PDR1/1, PDR1A/1, PDR1/2, PDR1/3, PDR2.1, AN68.1R, AN68.2R, AN68A.1R and AN68.2R. All had a 195 in. wheelbase except the PDR2.1, AN68.2R and AN68A.2R versions, whose wheelbases measured 222 in.

Although the 0.600 type 9.8 litre engine was initially employed in the Atlantean, the 0.680 version was introduced shortly afterwards and the PDR1/1 stayed in production until 1967, modern designs continuing, such as the AN68A/1 model as seen with the Roe bodied Atlanteans received by West Yorkshire in the early 1980s and those acquired by Southampton in 1982. The recent Atlantean AN68B.1R comes with a 16 ft. 3 in. wheelbase and overall length of 31 ft. 10 in. while the AN68B.2R has the larger 18 ft. 6 in. and 33 ft. 4 in. measurements, both buses having a gross vehicle weight of 15 tons. The AN68B.1R has an approximate turning circle of 56 ft. and the AN68B.2R one of 62 ft. The engine for these models is the Leyland 680 naturally aspirated six cylinder diesel unit and a Leyland five speed close ratio pneumo-cyclic gearbox and direct injection fuel system are further features. In 1968, British Holdings (which controlled Daimler) and Leyland merged. Leyland later ceased to use Daimler's system of chassis designation, the 30 ft. CRG6LX becoming the FE30GR, Chester City Transport being an example of an authority with FE30AGR buses.

TITAN The acclaimed Titan bus is built at Leyland's Workington plant and today many operators have examples of this high bridge double decker. The Titan's integral construction gives strength to the vehicle, permitting the transverse rear engine and gearbox to be suspended from the body shell without the need for a subframe. The famous TL11 in-line diesel engine is a six cylinder 11.1 litre four stroke turbocharged unit; a Gardener 6LXB 10.45 litre model is available as an option. The Leyland Hydrocyclic gearbox has an integral friction retarder to boost the braking system and is a five speed fully automatic model.

Passenger and driver comfort are of a high standard since the integral construction produces excellent vibration and noise isolation, as well as permitting a large interior with low floor and step height. The comfortable ride is helped by a good air suspension system giving roll control and stability, while driving controls, indicators, wipers, washers, horn and lights are within finger tip reach of the steering wheel rim. Furthermore, emergency red lights plus an audible buzzer alert the driver to faults such as low oil or brake operating pressure, while amber lights inform the driver of alternator problems and remind him if the handbrake is in use.

Several passenger authorities have purchased the Titan, including Reading Borough Transport and London whose vehicles began operating from Upton Park in April 1981.

OLYMPIAN The Olympian was the Leyland double decker of the early 1980s, a high or low bridge bus which proved to be popular with overseas markets such as China Motor Bus, a Hong Kong operator who acquired two Olympian/Eastern Coachwork vehicles in 1981. On the domestic market Alexander (Northern) received Olympian chassis in May 1981 while the Motor Show Olympian, 1451, went to Greater Manchester P.T.E. The versatile double deck chassis is also in service with Ribble, while Central S.M.T. (Scotland) had Alexander (Midland's) Olympian MRO1 on loan during 1981, and in 1982–83 Strathclyde P.T.E. received twenty Olympians, five with Eastern Coachworks bodies, the remainder carrying Roe bodywork.

The Olympian models ONTL 11/1R and ONLXB/1R have 9.6 m. wheelbases while the ONTL 11/2R and ONLXB/2R have 10.3 m. wheelbases. Customers have the choice of a Leyland TL11 six cylinder turbocharged engine with oil cooler or a Gardner 6LXB unit producing 177 bhp, and the impressive torque available over a wide engine speed range allows Olympian buses to achieve excellent performance figures. A vertical split dual circuit air system operates front and rear brakes, with a spring brake emergency blow off connection located at the front of the bus.

As usual, the steering is easy, being of a power assisted nature and the 9.66 m. vehicle manages an impressive turning circle of 19.8 m. (65 ft.) while the 10.3 m. bus can turn in 21.6 m. (71 ft.).

MAUDSLAY

The ML3 was one of several vehicles introduced by Maudslay during 1924, remaining in production until 1936. Following the Second World War the Warwickshire company brought out their Marathon Mark III chassis with a 17 ft. 7 in. wheelbase and an A.E.C. 7.7 litre oil engine, derated to give 98 bhp instead of 108 bhp. Hubert Hackets of Levenshulme, Manchester, was one of several private coach firms with a Marathon III. Foreign operators were offered an export version in the form of a chassis powered by an A.E.C. 9.6 litre engine and having either a 17 ft. 7 in. or 20 ft. wheelbase. MacBrayne, the Scottish firm, purchased sixteen Marathon IIIs with Park Royal and Croft bodywork, all first licensed in 1948, while the following year MacBrayne acquired a dozen more with C35F seating and Park Royal bodywork. In 1949 Maudslay was sold to A.E.C. although in later years the Reliance and Monocoach were advertised as Maudslay vehicles until the late 1950s.

A Maudslay Marathon Mark III displaying Whitson $1\frac{1}{2}$ deck bodywork.

M.C.W.

Metro-Cammell-Weymann (M.C.W.) produce the Metrobus as the 95 MDR and 11 MDR, the former being 31 ft. 4 in. long and 14 ft. 4¼ in. high, the latter having a length of 36 ft. 7 in. and height of 14 ft. 6 in. A Gardner 6LXB rated at 177 bhp at 1,850 rpm powers the 95 MDR, whilst a 6LXB rated at 188 bhp at 1,850 powers the 11 MDR. These Metrobuses seat seventy-three to seventy-seven people who benefit from full air suspension and more headroom than normal. Low body weight is ensured by using lightweight aluminium alloys in the body pillars and other structural components.

West Midlands, Greater Manchester P.T.E., London Transport and South Yorkshire are examples of authorities with M.C.W. buses. The early 1980s witnessed the delivery of three axle, 12 m. Super Metrobuses to the China Motor Bus Company and the Kowloon Motor Bus Company. The buses for Hong Kong have the Gardner 6LXCT turbocharged engine and a nominal capacity of one hundred and seventy passengers with sixty standing, while those in Kowloon are driven by Rolls-Royce engines. On the single decker market M.C.W. brought out a rear engined bus of integral construction using Swedish mechanical components from Scania Bussar, the bus division of Saab-Scania, and examples were found in the early 1970s with Leicester City Transport while London Transport acquired six vehicles, allocating them to Dalston, working alongside Leyland Nationals.

A Stockport based M.C.W. with Greater Manchester P.T.E. (above).

A three axle M.C.W. vehicle with the China Motor Bus Company (left).

MORRIS

In 1933 Birmingham Corporation Transport acquired three Morris-Commercial 'Imperial' double deckers. Four years later Morris introduced their Commercial CVF 13/5 semi-forward control chassis, powered by the company's six cylinder petrol engine. It stayed in production until 1950. Following the war, Morris-Commercial brought out a forward control thirty-two seat chassis with a 26 ft. overall length and a choice of engines including a Swiss Saurer model and a 3.8 litre Morris-Commercial unit, also employed in trucks. During 1952 the Austin and Morris groups combined and they stopped producing passenger chassis for domestic operators.

ROWE AND RUTLAND

The Cornish company of M. G. Rowe sold a number of Rowe Hillmaster single deckers to fleets in the south west. These underfloor engined buses possessed Meadows 4DC.330 oil engines at first and later 8.1 litre six cylinder models, or Gardner or A.E.C. engines. Mr. Rowe was, in fact, a coach operator and understood the need for coaches capable of negotiating the terrain peculiar to Devon and Cornwall, with most Rowe coaches boasting Whitson bodywork.

Motor Traction Ltd. of Surrey made the Rutland Clipper coach in 1954, a 30 ft. long single deck coach with a Perkins, Meadows or Gardner engine and Whitson bodywork.

SEDDON

MARK IV AND MARK VI In 1948 the Seddon firm introduced their Mark IV passenger chassis — the Marks I, II, III and V were goods vehicles. The Mark IV featured a main frame which was straight apart from a wheelarch, with a 16 ft. 6 in. wheelbase and either 7 ft. 6 in. or 8 ft. width. The engine range included units from Meadows, Gardner and A.E.C. The Mark VI of 1950 had similar specifications to its predecessor except that it had a wheelbase permitting the carriage of thirty-six people, while the Mark 6XR had a 17 ft. 10 in. wheelbase and a bigger Perkins engine.

PSV CHASSIS, 1952–59 The Mark 7P chassis appeared in 1952. The same year witnessed an underfloor engined bus with a vertical rather than horizontal engine and buses of this type were designated Mark 10P, 10R and Mark 11. The Marks 17, 18 and 19 came on the market between 1957 and 1959, the last two in the series featuring 16 ft. 4 in. wheelbases. Several overseas markets expressed an interest in Seddon vehicles, and Bermuda acquired Mark 10s with Pennine bodywork together with a batch in 1967 in pink livery.

OTHER SEDDON BUSES A variety of Seddon buses may be observed with several operators. The National Coal Board favoured the Seddon Midi bus in the mid 1970s while Greater Manchester P.T.E. employs Seddon/Pennine buses on the city centre 'Centre Line' service. Pennine VII buses serve with Scottish and Western, and Gosport and Fareham Omnibus Company had some Seddon's for stage carriage work in the late 1960s. During 1981, Eastern Scottish acquired Seddon/Pennine VII buses displaying Plaxton Supreme C49F coachwork.

A 1967 Seddon Pennine bus operating in Bermuda, finished in pink livery.

A one man operated Seddon with Pennine bodywork (1969) owned by Gosport and Fareham Omnibus Company.

SENTINEL

The first Sentinel passenger vehicle made its début in 1924 in the form of a thirty-two seat steam wagon with solid tyres and Hora bodywork. In the late 1930s Gilfords (HSG) Ltd. merged with Sentinel. The Gilford CF 176 chassis was supplied with a six cylinder petrol engine, receiving a Cowieson body in 1939, the final vehicle accommodating thirty-two passengers.

SENTINEL-BEADLE (SB) Having enjoyed some considerable success with underfloor engined lorries, Sentinel thought of using this type of engine in a bus design, such as those of B.M.M.O. passenger vehicles, and received help from the bodywork firm of Beadle in 1948. This Sentinel Beadle bus featured a light alloy body, the entrance positioned forward of the front axle, and an underfloor horizontal Sentinel 4D 6.08 litre four cylinder oil engine mounted behind the driver. With a 14 ft. 9 in. wheelbase this integrally constructed vehicle was 27 ft. long, carrying forty passengers. It was later renamed STC.

STC SERIES The coachwork in this series, although bearing a close resemblance to the former Beadle design, came from Sentinel. The STC4 had a 14 ft. 9 in. wheelbase, hydraulic servo brakes and room for forty people, power coming from a Sentinel four cylinder 6.08 litre horizontally mounted underfloor engine. Examples of this STC4/40 could be seen with Ribble Motor Services, Nickolls of Stafford and Maryland Coaches.

The year 1950 brought the introduction of longer Sentinel STC passenger vehicles, accomodating forty-four people and powered by a new 9.12 litre six cylinder $6SRH_2$ engine. An export chassis wheelbase measured 18 ft. 4 in., and the domestic model had an overall length of 30 ft. This STC6/44 bus exhibited a few modifications in body design, the offside windscreen, for instance, being angled inward. Examples were in operation with Ribble Motor Services and the Princess bus group in Newcastle. Three later models in the STC group included the STC4/27, STC6/30 and the STC6/33 with 14 ft. 9 in., 15 ft. 7 in. and 18 ft. 4 in. wheelbases, horizontal underfloor engines, a separate body construction, and the radiator mounted lower down than on earlier models.

SL SERIES Production of the SLC4 commenced in 1951. This 14 ft. 9 in. chassis had an overall length of 27 ft. 6 in. and had provision for conventional coachwork accommodating thirty-five passengers. Powered by a Sentinel 6.08 litre engine, the SLC4 had a five speed constant mesh gearbox, and servo-assisted brakes. Generally adopted for coach work in 1953, the SLC/30 chassis was powered by a direct injection Sentinel 6D engine, and had provision for a central entrance. Over seventy SLC chassis were produced. Companies utilising SLC buses included Best and Sons of Middlesex, Brown of Donnington Wood, and Trimdon Motor Services.

Acquired by Rolls-Royce in 1955, Sentinel stopped production of coaches and buses in 1956. Although only manufacturing in the region of one hundred and thirty buses for the domestic market, Sentinel can be remembered for manufacturing integral designed passenger vehicles with underfloor engines, modern features at the time.

SHELVOKE AND DREWRY

During 1981 the British Airports Authority received a prototype bus from Shelvoke and Drewry with Reeve Burgess body design featuring low entry and exit doors positioned centrally on both sides, seating for twenty-six people and a large luggage area. The drop frame chassis from Shelvoke facilitates such a bus. Power comes from a front mounted Ford 6 litre engine driving via an Albion four speed automatic gearbox. A deep windscreen affords good visibility, and passengers are provided with moquette covered seats. The bus is significant because it heralds the return to bus manufacturing of Shelvoke and Drewry after having been out of the bus business for some time, previous passenger vehicles including the E types of the late 1930s with rear mounted transverse engines, in service with Southdown Motor Services Ltd.

SUNBEAM

Prior to 1945 Sunbeam produced the three axle MS2 which also appeared with a Karrier nameplate. In 1948 Sunbeam was acquired from the Brockhouse Group by Guy who continued with Trolleybus manufacturing.

SUNBEAM S7 The S7 three axle trolleybus made an appearance in 1948, its dimensions being 18 ft. 6 in. wheelbase, 8 ft. wide and 30 ft. long. The S7A was a 7 ft. 6 in. option, and overseas buyers could purchase chassis with a 20 ft. wheelbase towards the end of the 1950s. A number of firms supplied bodywork for the S7 including Park Royal, East Lancashire Coachbuilders and Northern Coach Builders. Reading Corporation and Newcastle were examples of operators employing S7 vehicles.

MF2B A special chassis for use as a one man operated single deck trolleybus was introduced in 1950. Named the MF2B, its entrance was forward of the front axle, and it had allowance for an exit point at the rear or between the two axles. Overseas customers favoured the Sunbeam 17 ft.

6 in. and 18 ft. 6 in. wheelbase versions while U.K. operators used the 16 ft. 3 in. model. Kingston-upon-Hull requested short wheelbase MF2Bs equipped with Roe bodywork, for use as one man double deckers in 1953-54. Bournemouth received about forty between 1958 and 1962, the later models having Weymann H650 bodies; these, in fact, were among the last trolleybuses to be built for use in Britain.

SUNBEAM F4A The F4A came on the scene in 1952 with either 16 ft. 4 in., 17 ft. 6 in. or 18 ft. 6 in. wheelbases available. Some examples of early marques were seen in Walsall which acquired sixty-eight rear entrance trolleybuses with platform doors and Willowbrook bodywork. Reading, Derby and Belfast were among other operators in the United Kingdom who favoured F4A vehicles. Some of the world's biggest trolleybuses were, in fact, the twenty built by Sunbeam for use in Johannesburg, seating eighty-five in a vehicle 34 ft. long and 8 ft. 6 in. wide; bodywork came not only from Willowbrook but also from Roe, Burlingham and Harkness.

A 1959 Sunbeam MF2B with Weymann bodywork.

TILLING STEVENS

Thomas Tilling was one of the first fleet owners in London to employ motor buses in 1904 when he put a Milnes Daimler on the streets. Mr. Stevens had a tremendous interest in petrol electric vehicles and 1911 saw an agreement made between Tillings and W. A. Stevens for operating buses inside the Metropolitan Police area. Later developments included the Tilling Stevens TS3 chassis, the TS6 of 1924, the B10A of the following year, and a forward control chassis of 1932 with a four cylinder 5.13 litre engine.

K SERIES Tilling Stevens buses after 1945 were equipped with Gardner and Meadows engines. The K5LA7 bus was powered by a Gardner 5LW engine, while a 6LW version appeared with

K6LA7 vehicles Meadows 6DC630 engines provided power for the K6MA7 and K5MA9 buses, while a Meadows 4DC330 unit appeared with the L6PA7 prototype vehicle. Operators with K series coaches included Lanes, Neath and Cardiff, and Rhymney Transport. Bodywork was supplied by firms such as Duple, Theale and Longford.

The 1948 Commercial Motor Show was the scene for the announcement of an L type chassis with Perkins P6 engines, but it was not put into production, unlike the 1950 L type Express, termed the Express Mark II, which was powered by the Meadows 4DC330 5.4 litre four cylinder engine. Tilling Stevens was purchased by the Rootes group in 1950 but some buses continued to be produced until the mid 1950s.

THORNYCROFT

The Thornycroft Commercial and Military vehicle production commenced in 1864 under the auspices of John Thornycroft. Early passenger vehicles included the Thornycroft J of 1913, the BC Forward of 1927 and the Lightning of 1933 — a single deck coach with a 14 ft. 8 in. wheelbase. During the Second World War the firm produced Bren Gun Carriers and other military equipment, re-entering the bus market after the war.

BUSES AFTER 1945 Immediately after the war, Thornycroft experimented with YF/TR6 Sturdy twenty seat chassis, SG8 forward control chassis and two DG/NR6 chassis for use with

double deck bodywork, showing a large post war radiator.

The HF/ER4 Nippy forward control single decker was powered by a 3.9 litre Thornycroft four cylinder petrol engine and proved a popular choice for MacBraynes, having Harkness and Croft bodywork.

From 1950 Thornycroft concentrated on trucks and military vehicles. Some buses constructed for foreign markets, together with one or two in the U.K., employed lorry chassis, the Trident PG/CR6/1 chassis of 1957, featuring a 13 ft. 6 in. wheelbase and 5.5 litre diesel engine, being an example.

TROJAN AND VULCAN

A Trojan bus with a 7 ft. 10 in. wheelbase was constructed in 1953 with a Perkins engine. This Trojan DT vehicle was followed the next year by a 9 ft. 6 in. wheelbase bus capable of carrying twelve passengers, again powered by a

Perkins 3 engine. In 1949 the Vulcan single deck chassis appeared with a 15 ft. 3 in. wheelbase, popular only until the early 1950s, this bus having the Perkins P6 oil engine. The 6VF 13 ft. export chassis also came on the scene about this time.

FOREIGN BUSES ON U.K. ROADS

The arrival of foreign bus and coach chassis on the British market has resulted in a proliferation of passenger vehicle makes owned by British operators. However, foreign chassis frequently display British made coachwork. Fiat, Renault and the Magirus-Deutz M200 seem likely contenders for part of the British coach market in future years. Some of the more popular foreign marques have come from Volvo, Scania, D.A.F., M.A.N. and Mercedes. A selection of their vehicles common in Britain is considered.

D.A.F.

The 1950s saw D.A.F. commence with their production of bus chassis, designated B50 and BD50, 1958 being the era of the TB series chassis featuring a vertical front mounted engine.

The original D.A.F. demonstrator (JMK 554N) has been with Robinson's of Appleby for some time and the D.A.F. MB 200 (XPP 422S) was the first of its type in the U.K. carrying a Plaxton Supreme body.

MB 200 Companies in the United Kingdom running MB 200 coaches include Britannia Airways, Seamarks, Supreme Coaches, Sabre Coaches and Harris, Grays, Essex. Powered by a D.A.F. 1160 horizontal six cylinder turbocharged diesel engine, the MB 200 DKTL coach chassis is designed to form an integral unit with the body, and may be seen on the roads of the United Kingdom with bodywork provided by firms including Plaxton, Duple, Jonckheere and Van Hool.

SB 2005 DHU This chassis is powered by a D.A.F. 825 vertical six cylinder in-line turbocharged diesel engine, and is fitted with air suspension, front and rear stabilisers plus double acting telescopic shock absorbers on front and rear axles. Mounting the engine at the rear, plus a straight chassis frame, allows for a large luggage area to be provided between the axles, and thus makes the SB 2005 chassis ideal for coach work and inter city routes.

Van Hool bodywork on a D.A.F. 200 DKL coach.

M.A.N.

European operators employ many of the M.A.N. range which includes the CR 160, SR 240, SR 280, SL 200, the SG 220 18 metre articulated bus, and the SD-D three axled double decker bus with room for seventy-five seated passengers and fifty-four standing. In the United Kingdom, recent instances of operators with M.A.N. vehicles are Parks of Hamilton and N.A.T. Holidays of London, who possess a number of SR 280 coaches with seating for forty-nine together with washing and toilet facilities. The SR 280 is 11.45 m. long, has a 206 kW (280 hp) DIN, rear mounted engine and is ideal for long distances or excursions.

M.A.N. SR 280 coach featuring M.A.N. bodywork.

Mercedes

The vast range of Mercedes vehicles includes a number of passenger chassis employed by British fleet owners such as Luton Airport where passengers are transported in Mercedes-Benz 0 305 G articulated buses equipped by Lex Vehichle Engineering. The one thousandth Mercedes-Benz 0 305 G rear engined articulated bus was produced in 1981, the model having been on sale for three years. The smaller nineteen seat Devon Conversion Mercedes-Benz 508D bus is in production, coming with a 508D 3.8 litre OM 314 Mercedes diesel engine and five speed gearbox; Nadder Valley Coaches of Wiltshire is one company employing this vehicle. In the early 1980s, following some considerable time of selling only diesel light vans in Britain, Mercedes-Benz launched the 208 and 308 petrol engined chassis. With a top speed in excess of 70 mph and a minibus conversion by Devon with a 'hi-top' roof allowing full length luggage racks and wider seats than on earlier models, this vehicle is available with either petrol or diesel engines.

The Mercedes-Benz 0305G/Lex Engineering articulated bus, 1980.

Scania

Scania's experience of rear engine buses goes back to the 1950s when Stockholm wanted to renew its passenger vehicle fleet. In conjunction with Mack, Scania designed a bus whose frame and bodywork were built as integral units with direct mounted engine, transmission and controls. In recent years the Scania 112 range came on the market featuring models such as the articulated BR 112A and the CR 112 with forty-eight seats and many safety features.

BR 112H The Birmingham Motor Show of 1980 was the scene for the inauguration of Scania's double decker with East Lancashire bodywork. With transverse rear mounted engine and excel-

A Scania double decker carrying East Lancashire Coachbuilders bodywork, 1980.

lent facilities for driver and passenger alike, the noise level is about 77 dB (A), the same as that of a family car, the engine compartment having a separate ventilator and fan. The radiator is thermostatically controlled, while all round air suspension together with six adjustable shock absorbers guarantees a comfortable and stable ride. During mid 1981 and early 1982 Newport Borough Transport received about a dozen BR 112H double deckers with Marshall bodies, carrying seventy-five seated passengers on the short wheelbase chassis with Voith D851 transmission. Current trends indicate further sales of this double decker to other U.K. operators in the mid 1980s, as typified by the Gibson (Leicester) group who have BR 112DHs with eighty seats.

Newport Transport's double deck Scania BR112H vehicle with Marshall coachwork.

A 1981 Volvo B58 equipped with Duple Dominant III bodywork.

Volvo

The Volvo name is legendary in the area of reliability and precision engineering, manifest in all Volvo's output whether trucks, agricultural products, fire engines, or their famous cars. This same excellence displays itself in the impressive range of Volvo coaches and buses. Countries such as Denmark have examples of Volvo coaches with forty-five seat Jonckheere bodywork, while U.K. operators can boast Volvos with coachwork by firms such as Alexander, Duple and Plaxton.

B10 The Volvo bus programme has included a mid engined bus since 1951, the company making more than twenty thousand such vehicles, with the recent B10M proving a popular choice for continental and U.K. fleets. Powered by a turbocharged horizontal, six cylinder in-line diesel engine, the B10M comes with a choice of eight gearboxes and two options for final drive, air brakes on three circuits — front axle, rear axle,

and parking brake — while the large luggage compartment is facilitated by the chassis layout. The mid mounted engine ensures a centre of gravity in the middle and the B10M is ideal as an articulated bus with three axles.

Examples of U.K. companies favouring the B10 are Wallace Arnold who use them on several routes including the London–Moscow run, these having Plaxton bodies, Cotters of Scotland with Van Hool bodied buses and G.K. Kinch, whose Plaxton Viewmaster executive bodied B10M won the Coach of the Year Award at the 1981 Brighton coach rally, the same operator also having won the 1980 event by entering a Volvo B58 with Plaxton Supreme IV bodywork. Duple Dominant III bodied B10Ms for Western S.M.T. are popular on the Glasgow-London route, making their first appearance in 1981.

B58 A long wheelbase, mid positioned engine and wide spread axles gives the B58 excellent stability. Power comes from Volvo's six cylinder four stroke diesel engine with direct injection combustion chambers. The B58–56 boasts a turning circle of 60 ft., the B58–61 one of 64.3 ft. The popularity of Volvo B 58s with U.K. operators is reflected by the increasing number of fleets putting this vehicle on the road, such as A1 of Ardrossan and Allander, Scotland, the former having a B58–56 with Van Hool C51F body, the latter preferring Duple C53F coachwork on their B58 which was purchased in 1980. Clyde Coast Volvo B58s carry Duple Dominant III coachwork while examples of Dominant II bodywork may be observed on B58s owned by Coliseum of Southampton, and PG Travel of Middlewich. Plaxton bodywork is also found on Volvos such as on a B58–61 which Boons of Boreham acquired in 1981. It is interesting to note that the one thousandth B58 to be handed over in the U.K. since its introduction had a Plaxton body. It is owned by Berkeley Coach and Travel of Paulton.

Fifty-seven seat Duple Dominant II coachwork on a Volvo B58 12 metre coach.

142

AILSA MARK III DOUBLE DECKER The repute of Volvo single deckers encouraged the company to put their Ailsa double decker on the U.K. market with some impressive results, made possible by excellent technical specifications, road handling, quality engineering and passenger comfort. A semi-integral double deck underframe with Volvo TD 70H front mounted engine, the Ailsa has a five speed Wilson gearbox and an all welded sealed box section frame with a channel peripheral frame, protected by the renowned Volvo undersealants and paints. Many authorities have shown an interest in the Ailsa Mark III, including Manchester, and West Midlands, and the early 1980s saw Strathclyde P.T.E. take delivery of thirty or so Mark IIIs with Alexander R type coachwork, featuring black lower deck window surrounds and black vinyl seats. In 1983 even more operators began negotiations for the Ailsa.

One of the Volvo Ailsa double deckers with Alexander 'R' bodywork, acquired by Strathclyde P.T.E. during the early 1980s.

INDEX

ACKNOWLEDGEMENTS The majority of illustrations are from the John Creighton Collection. The author would like to thank companies and acquaintances who assisted with further material.